Cybersecurity and Privacy Law

Introduction

ConvoCourses

medical, or professional advice. The content within this book has been derived from various sources. Please consult a licensed professional before attempting any techniques outlined in this book.

By reading this document, the reader agrees that under no circumstances is the author responsible for any losses, direct or indirect, that are incurred as a result of the use of the information contained within this document, including, but not limited to, errors, omissions, or inaccuracies.

Check us out:

http://convocourses.com

youtube.com/convocourses

Contact us:

contact@convocourses.com

Table of Contents

Chapter 1: Fundamentals of Cybersecurity and Privacy Laws

On January 29th, 2015, Anthem Blue Cross Blue Shield admitted to a data breach that affected over 78 million people, employees and their customers included. Anthem reported this breach, where a lot of customer information was leaked. It was reported that one of their database administrators discovered that their credentials were being used without their knowledge and consent. This unauthorized access led to the breach of consumer information, including but not limited to member names, member health identification numbers, dates of birth, Social Security numbers, addresses, telephone numbers, email addresses, employment information, and income data. Because Anthem is a health insurance company, the exposed data directly violated the Health Insurance Portability and Accountability Act (HIPAA). There was a consolidated class-action lawsuit, i.e., a case was made on behalf of many people against Anthem. This class action was settled in 2018 for a sum of $115 million. Anthem collaborated with the FBI and a private security agency to track down the hackers and was able to trace them to a few Chinese nationals. No evidence suggested that the breach had led to identity fraud, and Anthem maintained they were not violating data security laws. This incident almost ten years ago suggests that there has long since been a need for better-defined cybersecurity laws to protect our digital assets.

More data breaches have violated various security and privacy laws in recent years. Notably, the Equifax leak in 2017, where the financial and personal information of more than 150 million people was lost because of a known Apache vulnerability, which was left unpatched. The company had to make massive settlements with the Federal Trade Commission (FTC), the Consumer Financial Protection Bureau (CFPB), and all 50 U.S. states and territories. All because they were negligent in maintaining and updating their devices and software. Hacks on the Democratic National Party during the 2016 elections were a serious breach of privacy and cybersecurity laws. These are only a few examples of law violations caused by data breaches. Another gross violation of privacy by design occurred when Facebook came under scrutiny for selling user data to the analytics company Cambridge Analytica. While Facebook faced lawsuits and fines by the FTC and SEC. It also raised a lot of ethical questions. The need for better and well-defined laws was deeply felt after this incident in 2018. Along with these laws, a need for better enforcement of said laws, as well as awareness of cyber laws, became an essential part of the path forward.

Over the past decade, as the number of incidents has risen, it has become amply clear that there is a need to regulate how things are handled in the digital world. Users' personal information has become a sought-after entity; we need stricter rules to protect the privacy and security of the customers. As countries recognize this need, there have been numerous Acts and Laws that different governments have implemented to ensure proper security and privacy measures are in place whenever a company handles customer or other sensitive data.

Just like the existence of these laws is important, awareness and proper implementation from the management level to the implementation level are also equally important. This book is written with that in mind. This book aims to make its readers aware of the most important data security and privacy laws in play today and how they apply to different organizations providing different functions in the industry. Accordingly, in the book's first part, we'll discuss the basic principles behind these laws and how they affect the tech industry, introducing readers to standards that help make organizations compliant with cyber law. Standards like the NIST 800 Risk Management Framework. NIST 800 provides a structured approach for managing security and privacy risks within an organization by implementing a continuous monitoring process. We'll also talk about the most common security laws in the US today.

Next, we talk about the different cyber laws across the globe and how, despite the laws being for a different countries, they can also affect data handling practices in other countries. Given how interconnected the online world is, this is a natural consequence. We discuss laws specific to the healthcare industry, the payment card industry, and publicly traded companies. We'll also discuss cyber laws in government organizations like DoD and NASA.

This book will discuss privacy laws and how they can differ from cyber laws. We'll provide practical information on implementing these laws in organizations. We will also cover how certifications for specific laws and regulations can enhance your security posture while at the same time helping organizations abide by the said laws. We hope to provide a comprehensive guide to important cyber and privacy laws, their role in everyday industry functioning, and how to incorporate them into your work to remain compliant while providing the best product or service for your customers.

What are Cyber Laws

When we think of law enforcement in the digital world, a natural question arises: What are cyber laws? Cyber laws encompass the legal aspects of any activities and interactions that happen in cyberspace. This includes communications and transactions over networked devices and the distribution and storage of data and information. For this book, we only talk about the abstract or "digital" aspect of cybersecurity and not the physical machines and connections where the digital world lives. These laws exist to ensure all actions happening on the internet are ethical and authorized by all parties involved in the action. They are designed to protect both the individual as well as the organization. Cyber laws protect against three types of cybercrime: crimes against people, property, and government.

Crimes Against People

These are the most common types of cybercrime where the target is to defraud people on the internet and to either cause them harm or gain something from them, or both. These include crimes ranging from cyberbullying, stalking, and harassment to credit card theft, identity theft, and human trafficking.

Crimes Against Property

Crimes against property are those cyber crimes that target devices on the internet like servers, routers, firewalls, etc. For most hacking activities, crime against property is a byproduct of the actual purpose of the hack, which is usually to disrupt normal function or steal information to inconvenience end-users. Common types of this crime are Denial of Service (DOS) attacks, computer viruses, exploiting network vulnerabilities like the Dyn DNS attack, etc.

Crimes Against Government

These types of crimes are more specific and target nation-state vectors to disrupt a nation's defense systems to either cause fear and panic, gain confidential national security information, or even facilitate physical attacks.

With comprehensive and well-enforced cyber laws, the idea is to protect against these most commonly seen cyber crimes.

Privacy Laws

Privacy laws generally fall under cyber laws but deserve to be discussed separately because of how much they affect the entire cyber landscape. Privacy laws predominantly apply to the privacy of individual people on the internet. These laws dictate how a user's personal information is obtained, stored, and used. An important factor is how this information is processed and shared with third-party organizations, which may use this data for marketing, analytics, or something else. As hackers focus on the easier target of user personal information, privacy laws and enforcement of privacy laws become increasingly important. With the rise of new privacy laws, some data collection, processing, and storage fundamentals remain common. These privacy fundamentals include consent, purpose, disclosure, and security practices.

Consent

Consent is at the forefront of privacy laws. It is the process by which end users grant permission for organizations to collect, store, or process their data. This is imperative to ensure that the data collection is transparent and ethical.

Key Aspects of Consent:

Explicit Consent: Users must actively give permission, usually via a distinct action like ticking a box. Pre-ticked boxes or any form of assumed consent aren't considered valid in many jurisdictions.

Informed Consent: Users must be provided with clear and comprehensive information about what data will be collected and how it will be used.

Revocability: The users should be able to withdraw their consent at any given time.

Purpose

The purpose of data collection is another pillar of privacy. Data shouldn't be gathered without a clear, predefined reason.

Key Aspects of Purpose:

Specificity: The reasons for collecting data should be specific and not overly broad.

Legitimate Reasons: Organizations should only collect personal data for genuine, legitimate purposes and not for malicious intent.

No Excessive Data: Only the necessary data for the expressed purpose should be collected. Superfluous data collection without clear reasoning is frowned upon.

Disclosure

Disclosure revolves around transparency. It emphasizes the importance of organizations being open about their use of personal data.

Key Aspects of Disclosure:

Transparency: Organizations must be transparent about how they plan to use the data.

Third-party Sharing: Any intentions to share user data with third-party entities should be clearly stated.

Duration: Organizations should inform users how long they intend to keep their data.

Security Practices

Information on the security practices and procedures followed by the data collection organization.

Ensuring that collected data is secure is vital. With the rise of cyber threats, robust security practices are a non-negotiable aspect of data privacy.

Key Aspects of Security Practices:

Data Encryption: This involves encoding data to prevent unauthorized access. Data should be encrypted both in transit and at rest.

Regular Audits: Organizations should conduct security audits to identify and fix potential vulnerabilities.

Access Control: It is essential to limit who can access the data and ensure that only authorized personnel can view or process it.

Breach Notification: In the event of a data breach, organizations must have procedures in place to notify affected users and relevant authorities promptly.

These fundamental rules are part of most privacy policies applied by organizations as a result of the privacy laws. Like cyber laws, privacy laws also can vary between countries, and based on where the data is stored and handled, privacy laws from a different country may be applied to data in another country.

Privacy Laws Vs. Security Laws

While it may be that privacy laws fall generally under cyber laws, there are differences. Security laws mainly focus on protecting all the data that an organization has, whereas privacy laws focus on managing personally identifiable information (PII), points of data that can be used to accurately identify a specific person. Security laws dictate how we store, transmit, and maintain data within an organization; this includes whether data is encrypted, different access control measures, etc. Privacy regulations dictate what PII data is collected, how we collect it, how it is being used in the organization, and who we share it with.

As you can see, there is a lot of overlap. One can argue that they can be considered the same, but their approach towards regulations is the biggest difference. Security is data-focused; it will protect whatever data falls under the regulation. Privacy is user-focused to protect real end users online. However, they are deeply interconnected, and one only strengthens the other.

Here is an example to understand the nuanced difference between the two: when a data breach occurs where hackers forcibly access or steal information, we consider security laws violated. But, if information or data is shared voluntarily by an organization without the knowledge of the user whose information is being shared, it would be considered a violation of privacy laws.

Why Do We Need Security And Privacy Laws?

The internet can be very autonomous, offering little in terms of regulations or behavior guidelines. We interact with people's data and websites from all around the world daily over the internet. Similarly, malicious actors can sit in any corner of the world and affect people. Because of this internet structure, it can be difficult to understand and apply rules and regulations. The internet can seem like a fully virtual space, but with the increasing intersection of the internet with our physical lives, any disruption online can affect our lives seriously. With things like banking, shopping, education, contract agreements, and more happening online, a hack or a data breach can really impact our lives. As cyber-attacks increased and their after-effects became life-altering, a need to demarcate jurisdictions and apply laws for protecting everyday online activities is very real.

As the number of users online and the involvement of citizens in online activities differs from country to country, different governments apply their laws for data protection and handling. Because of differences in culture and mindsets, the strictness of laws, especially privacy laws, can vary quite a bit. With time, it was understood that organizations from different industries interacted differently with data. The social media industry thrived on sharing people's data, whereas the healthcare industry needed strict confidentiality of an individual's data. Looking at this, some new laws were enforced with regulations specific to the industry they were applied to. As laws and regulations became more and more common across the internet, the cybersecurity industry had to adapt.

Impact of Cyber Laws

Impact On Industry

Cyber Laws have had a two-sided impact on the tech industry. On the one hand, it provides individuals and organizations a way to seek justice and compensation for damages in a cyber attack. On the other hand, it requires organizations and the industry, in general, to adhere to stricter rules and be more organized in their approach to security.

Because of cyber security laws, industries that deal with sensitive data, like banking, finance, etc., have to uphold higher security standards in following these rules. E-commerce industries have started accessing more sensitive information from their users and are rapidly beginning to fall under the categories where higher security laws need to be followed. The need to follow security laws has introduced the concept of compliance within the tech industry. Having compliance, or being compliant, implies that a company or organization is in a state where it is following all the rules and regulations set upon the industry by the responsible legislative bodies. In many major companies, compliance has become a separate department unto itself to ensure a particular product or service is running in accordance with the established regulations.

Nevertheless, having a compliance department is insufficient to know if a company adheres to the laws, nor does it automatically ensure compliance requirements are met. Because of this, third-party reviews have been introduced to ensure all the regulations are properly followed and implemented. These reviews are called compliance audits conducted by authorized external organizations on companies. The audit reports measure risk management, thoroughness of compliance preparations, user access controls, and so forth based on what type of company it is and what data it gathers, stores, and/or transmits. Apart from these external compliance audits, internal audits are also performed within the company to ensure the organization follows both external and internal guidelines, and these reports can be used to improve a company's compliance posture iteratively.

Impact on People

Cyber laws have also had a social impact on the world. With cybercrime on the rise, more and more people have faced its negative effects and, therefore, have become vigilant about cybercrime and cyber laws. With stricter standards in the industry in general, there has been a shift in how data is collected and used, which has also seen its impact on the people. New rules on password creation, use, recovery, and two-factor authentication have become commonplace, along with various other security standards applied based on the industry. With rising awareness, end-users have also increased the use of security products like anti-virus software and virtual private networks (VPNs). Overall, there has been a shift towards better security practices within the user community.

Intellectual Property

When discussing cyber laws, it's relevant to discuss intellectual property (IP) law and how it applies to technology. While it doesn't directly correlate to cybersecurity, IP must be protected when discussing cybercrime and online theft. In the digital world, some of the assets where IP rights can be applied are:

Copyright
These protect any asset that can be transmitted over the internet, including but not limited to music, movies, books, blogs, etc.

Patents
There can be two types of patents in the digital world. It can be either for a new software or business methodology; IP rights protect both.

Trademarks
Trademarks are used the same way online as in the physical world and are mostly used to protect websites.

Domain Disputes

Domains here refer to the web addresses used by any website, and owners of said domains can invoke IP rights in case of any dispute for the domain.

These are examples of how IP rights are applied in the digital world. Many other digital assets can be protected under IP rights, which are beyond the scope of this book. In case it is unclear whether a particular aspect of the system or business function is covered by IP law, it is best to consult a legal team specializing in cyber and IP law.

Chapter 2: Key U.S. Cybersecurity Laws and Regulations

To know exactly which control needs to be applied to remain within legal boundaries and in compliance with security and privacy requirements, this chapter focuses on some of the most common cybersecurity and privacy laws in practice in the United States.

Federal Information Security Modernization Act (FISMA)

What is FISMA?

The Federal Information Security Modernization Act (FISMA) was enacted as a part of the E-Government Act of 2002. It establishes regulations for federal data security standards and guidelines. FISMA requires all federal government agencies, even those not involved in national security, to develop, document, and implement an information security program. This program is designed to protect sensitive data and the information systems supporting agency operations and assets. These requirements extend to assets managed by another agency, third-party vendors, or service providers.

These agencies must also perform annual reviews to

determine the efficacy of the implemented data and information system protections. It has since expanded to include state agencies administering federal programs as well.

FISMA 2014

The replacement of FISMA 2002 with FISMA 2014 deserves to be mentioned as it brought to the forefront the need to emphasize data and systems protection within the federal systems. According to the Federal Information Security Modernization Act, this replacement updated the practices by:

- Codifying the Department of Homeland Security (DHS) authority to administer the implementation of information security policies for non-national security federal Executive Branch systems, including providing technical assistance and deploying technologies to such systems;
- Amending and clarifying the Office of Management and Budget's (OMB) oversight authority over federal agency information security practices and by
- Requiring OMB to amend or revise OMB A-130 to "eliminate inefficient and wasteful reporting."

The National Institute of Standards and Technology developed the standards and guidelines for all federal agencies to protect their systems and information.

It works closely with federal agencies to improve their understanding and implementation of FISMA.

FISMA Requirements

FISMA determines many organization requirements, but an agency must comply with seven main requirements:

Information System Inventory

FISMA requires agencies and third-party vendors to identify all the information systems and maintain an inventory; this includes any interfaces the systems interact with, including those not controlled by the agency itself.

Risk Categorization

All assets, data, and systems need to be categorized based on the risk they pose and the number of security controls they may need for a range of risk levels.

Security Controls

FISMA emphasizes the importance of security controls but does not delve into their specifics. Instead, it mandates federal agencies to implement necessary controls, drawing guidance primarily from the National Institute of Standards and Technology (NIST). To aid agencies, NIST's Special Publication 800-53 offers an extensive catalog of potential security and privacy controls. However, agencies are not required to apply all these controls; they are to implement only those deemed essential based on their specific risk assessment and operational needs.

Risk Assessment

Risk Assessments are a very important aspect of determining an agency's security and privacy posture when we start adding controls. It is even more important to conduct these assessments on an ongoing basis to evaluate the effectiveness of the implemented risk management. Potential cyber threats, cyberattacks, vulnerabilities, exploits, and other common attack vectors must be identified and mapped to controls designed to mitigate them. Then, the risk is determined based on the likelihood and impact of a scenario based on the existing controls.

System Security Plan (SSP)

FISMA mandates that federal agencies maintain thorough documentation of their security controls. Central to this requirement is the System Security Plan (SSP), which provides a detailed record of the security measures in place for a particular system. The SSP should be regularly reviewed and updated to reflect changes in the system and its environment. It serves not only as a reference for the agency but also as a crucial component during the security assessment and authorization processes. The plan's accuracy and completeness are critical, as it is evaluated against the guidance provided by the NIST to ensure that the chosen and implemented controls adhere to recommended standards and best practices. NIST SP 800-18 describes the content that should be in an SSP.

Certifications and Accreditations

FISMA underscores the significance of certification and accreditation to validate that security controls are properly implemented and risks are mitigated to an acceptable level. Accreditation is a formal declaration by an agency official, indicating they acknowledge and accept the security postures of their systems, and thus can be held accountable for any breaches or lapses. To facilitate the intricate process of certification and accreditation, NIST Special Publication 800-37 offers a structured framework, providing federal agencies with detailed steps, procedures, and best practices to ensure a thorough and consistent approach.

Continuous Monitoring

Continuous monitoring is an important requirement of FISMA. Monitoring is to ensure ongoing security and compliance of federal information systems. For a system to be FISMA accredited, it isn't just about initial implementation; the system must be regularly observed, with any significant changes or updates documented. When these modifications occur, they may necessitate a reassessment to guarantee continued adherence to security requirements and to identify potential vulnerabilities. This proactive approach helps in maintaining the system's security posture and in responding swiftly to emerging threats or changes.

Implementing the FISMA requirements across all federal systems relies heavily on the National Institute of Standards and Technology guidelines, which are discussed in greater detail in the next chapter.

Benefits and Penalties

FISMA has significantly improved federal agencies' security and privacy posture and allowed them to eliminate vulnerabilities cost-effectively.

A benefit to private agencies is that FISMA compliance significantly improves their likelihood of getting a federal contract with the side effect of improving their security in the process.

For government agencies and third-party agencies working with them, failing to meet FISMA compliance can result in reduced funding, reputation damage, congressional censure, and government hearings, among other drawbacks.

Best Practices

Some of the best practices to follow to easily obtain and maintain FISMA compliance are:

- Classify information as it is generated to easily identify and prioritize risk mitigation.
- Encrypt sensitive data at rest and in transit.
- Run regular risk assessments.
- Conduct employee training and education.
- Maintain evidence of what your organization is doing to achieve compliance.
- Be up-to-date with the latest changes to rules and regulations.

Computer Fraud and Abuse Act (CFAA)

The Computer Fraud and Abuse Act (CFAA) is a US federal law created in 1986 to amend the first federal computer fraud law, the 1984 Comprehensive Crime Control Act. The CFAA primarily addresses the issue of hacking or unauthorized access to computers, especially those owned by the federal government and financial institutions. Still, its applications have been broadened over time.

Originally, the CFAA targeted particularly federal computer crimes, such as attacks on government computers. However, its scope has expanded over the years due to various amendments. Now, it covers a wide range of computer activities, which can sometimes encompass seemingly benign activities if they involve unauthorized or exceed authorized access.

The CFAA has attracted criticism and controversy, primarily due to its broad language and the perception that it can be used to prosecute relatively trivial offenses. Critics argue that some of its provisions are overly vague, which can lead to disproportionate penalties for minor infractions.

Violations of the CFAA can lead to both criminal and civil penalties. Criminal penalties range from misdemeanors to felonies, depending on the nature and consequences of the offense. In some circumstances, violators can face substantial fines and imprisonment.

Over the years, the CFAA has been the subject of numerous court cases, and its interpretation has evolved. Some courts have taken a broad view of what constitutes "unauthorized access" or "exceeding authorized access," while others have adopted a narrower perspective.

The CFAA remains a critical piece of legislation for addressing computer-related crimes in the U.S.. Still, its application and interpretation have been, and continue to be, the subject of debate and litigation.

Some key provisions of the CFAA include:

- **Unauthorized Access to a Computer:** This includes accessing without authorization the computers of the U.S. government, financial institutions, and any computer used in or affecting interstate or foreign commerce.

- **Exceeding Authorized Access:** This means that someone had permission to access the computer, but they went beyond the limits of that permission (for example, by accessing data they weren't supposed to).

- **Transmitting Harmful Code:** It's an offense under the CFAA to knowingly transmit a program, code, or command that causes harm to a computer, its data, or its systems.

- **Fraud:** If someone accesses a computer without (or beyond) authorization and, by doing so, obtains something of value, they can be charged under the CFAA.

- **Trafficking in Passwords:** Knowingly selling or otherwise distributing passwords to a computer can be a violation. This is done a lot on the Dark Web.

- **Damaging a Computer or Information:** This section applies to those who cause damage through unauthorized access or transmitting harmful code.

The Department of Justice (DOJ) has guidelines and policies that federal prosecutors can use when determining whether to bring charges under various statutes, including the CFAA. These are not directly part of the CFAA but are part of the DOJ's broader prosecutorial discretion. They can clarify which cases are prioritized and how the law should be applied in different circumstances (see https://www.justice.gov/ for more).

Privacy Act of 1974

The US Privacy Act of 1974 allows individuals to access

records about themselves. It applies to federal organizations collecting data on people. It restricts the government's ability to collect information about citizens. It controls how they collect information, how it is maintained, used, and published. Its purpose is to give rights to the individuals whose data is collected. It protects individuals against unwarranted invasions of privacy.

Some of the main features of the Privacy Act are:

- Consent of individuals whose information is collected.
- Transparency in the collection and use of the information.
  Protection of the records being collected.

Federal organizations meet the requirements of this law by creating banners on sites collecting data to inform users and by issuing a "System of Records Notice (SORN)," which is a public notification that documents the purpose of a system of records. A system of records is a group of records controlled by an agency.

Freedom of Information Act

The Freedom of Information Act (FOIA), inaugurated on July 5, 1967, stands as a testament to the United States' commitment to transparency and the empowerment of its citizenry. Envisioned as a tool to strengthen democratic engagement, it affirms every citizen's right to seek and access information held within the confines of the US federal government's various departments. A visit to FOIA.gov serves as the portal through which individuals can exercise this right, demystifying the operations and decisions of governmental entities. While FOIA is anchored in the ethos of openness, it is also pragmatic. Recognizing the need for security and privacy, the act includes specific exemptions, ensuring that information which could jeopardize national security, infringe on personal privacy, or hinder governmental functions remains protected. Thus, while promoting transparency, FOIA also respects the boundaries essential for effective governance and the safeguarding of the nation's interests.

Cybersecurity Information Sharing

Act (CISA)

What is CISA?

In the cybersecurity profession, we often associate the acronym CISA with the Cybersecurity & Infrastructure Security Agency (CISA.gov). But in cybersecurity law, "CISA" stands for the Cybersecurity Information Sharing Act. The CISA act was made into law in December 2015. This law's main objective is to enhance cybersecurity in the U.S. through improved collaboration between private entities and the federal government. It provides two primary provisions for companies: First, it permits companies to implement specific monitoring and defensive measures to safeguard their data and information systems. Second, it offers incentives, like protection from liability and protection from Freedom of Information Act (FOIA) disclosure, to motivate companies to voluntarily share cyber threat indicators and defensive measures with the federal government, state and local governments, and even other private entities. To qualify for these protections, any shared data must have irrelevant personal information removed to ensure the privacy of individuals is upheld.

The Key provisions under this law are:

Monitor and Defend Information Systems

It allows companies and organizations to monitor their information systems and defend them against threats while protecting them from the liability of monitoring the said data and systems.

Mutual sharing of threat indicators and Defensive measures

Under this, a company can share and receive information about cyber threat indicators and defensive measures to federal, state, and local governments, other companies, and private entities.

Scrubbing of Personal Information

Any information about threat indicators or defense measures that will be shared should be scrubbed of all PII.

Protections for Sharing Information (As Applicable)

Protection from liability. There is no liability for sharing and receiving relevant information.

- Antitrust exemption. Companies aren't considered in violation of trust if they share properly scrubbed relevant information or receive such information.

- Non-waiver of privilege. Companies are not considered in violation of privilege

> and legal protections when they share threat data or defensive measures.
> - Information shared under CISA is exempt from disclosure under the FOIA.
> - This information cannot be used to regulate or take action against lawful activities.

Other requirements and provisions include restrictions on the sharing and use of data, implementation of security controls, voluntary participation, and the proper use of data by the federal government.

Federal Guidance for the Private Sector

The Department of Homeland Security (DHS) and the Department of Justice (DOJ) have released guidelines on what data can and cannot be shared under the act.

Information that may be shared

Information about threat actors. For example, information on new phishing techniques, analysis of a new piece of malware, a vulnerability found in software, or an attack a company faces.

Information about the defensive measures a company is using. For example, a new computer program, a new malware signature, or an AI technique for malware detection etc.

Information that may not be shared

A company should not share procedures for removing

personal information. They can do an internal assessment of how and what they are scrubbing.

Protected Health information, human resources information, consumer or transaction histories, and financial information are examples of information that must not be shared.

Implications and Recommendations

The broader idea behind CISA is to encourage information sharing between companies and the government. This provides everyone involved with a larger pool of information that can help them equip themselves to better defend against certain crimes overall.

Because of the legal protections provided under CISA, there is a greater motivation for all companies to share at least the baseline level of data and information.

In sharing such information, a company should consider the impact of a cyber threat and the cost and benefit of sharing such information. They should also make a realistic assessment of the strengths and limitations of the government protections. They should implement procedures to determine, collect, process, and share the information.

Gramm-Leach-Bliley Act (GLBA)

What is GLBA?

The Gramm-Leach-Bliley Act (GLBA), also known as the Financial Modernization Act of 1999, is a law that applies to financial institutions. According to this law, all financial institutions must explain how they share and protect their users' data. They must inform their customers about handling the collected personal data and grant them the right to opt-out of certain information sharing. As a documented security plan outlines, they must also implement specific protection measures for the collected customer data. This act comprises two rules and one provision.

Financial Privacy Rule:

Financial institutions or companies that receive non-public personal information from such institutions must adhere to this rule. This encompasses most personal information, such as names, dates of birth, and Social Security numbers, as well as transactional data like card and bank account numbers. Furthermore, it includes any personal data acquired during a transaction.

Safeguards Rule:

This rule mandates that companies protect private information under the GLBA. Firms must have both physical and technological means to securely collect, store, transmit, and process their customers' personal information. This involves having appropriate software, routinely testing vulnerabilities, and training employees to safeguard private data.

Pretexting Provisions:
This provision dictates that financial institutions must put measures in place to prevent unauthorized access to data.

Benefits of GLBA

For financial institutions, GLBA compliance results in fewer penalties and a reduced risk of reputational damage. Customers also benefit, as their personal information is better protected and safeguarded. No personal data can be collected without their knowledge and consent, and all user activity is monitored to prevent unauthorized or suspicious access or data leaks.

Potential GLBA Penalties

According to De Groot (Digital Guardian, 2023), if case non-compliance is proven, it can have life-altering effects that include:

- Financial institutions found in violation face fines of $100,000 for each violation.
- Individuals in charge found in violation face fines of $10,000 for each violation.
- Individuals found in violation can be imprisoned for up to 5 years.

Best Practices

To protect customer data, an institution must have an information security plan in place that is tailored to the kind of data they collect, the size of their organization, how they store and process data, and so forth. According to the Safeguards Rule, as mentioned by De Groot (2023), covered financial institutions must:

- Designate one or more employees to coordinate its information security program.
- Identify the risks to customer information in each area of the company's operation and evaluate the effectiveness of the current safeguards for controlling these risks.
- Chosen service providers must apply and maintain safeguards to the data; it should be part of the contract, and the institutions must ensure the safeguards are maintained.
- Evaluate and adjust the program in light of changing circumstances in business and the threat landscape.

California Consumer Privacy Act (CCPA)

What is CCPA?

The California Consumer Privacy Act (CCPA) is a law that provides personal information rights to all residents of California. Beyond consumers of household goods and services, this act also extends rights to individuals employed, engaged in independent contract-based employment, and other members of the workforce, as well as contacts from business customers or vendors based in California.

Under the CCPA, "personal information" is defined broadly as any data that directly or indirectly identifies relates to, or can be reasonably linked with a consumer or household.

You might think the CCPA applies to all entities in California collecting personally identifiable information, but it only applies to organizations that hit certain requirements. The CCPA's requirements apply to for-profit entities doing business in California that collect consumers' personal information and meet any of the following thresholds:

- Annual gross revenue exceeding $25 million (adjusted for inflation).
- Annually buying, receiving, sharing, or selling the personal information of over 50,000 consumers, households, or devices for commercial purposes.
- Deriving 50% or more of their annual revenues from selling consumers' personal information.

Exceptions to CCPA

The CCPA has specific exceptions, including:

- Business needs such as sharing information during mergers or acquisitions.
- Conflicts of law scenarios, like defending against legal claims, cooperating with law enforcement, or complying with other applicable regulations.
- Jurisdictional situations, for example, if all transactions and business operations occur entirely outside of California, or if another data privacy regulation, like Health Insurance Portability and Accountability Act, applies.

Consumer Rights under CCPA

Under the CCPA, consumers have the right to:

- Know how a business collects, stores, uses, and shares personal information.
- Request the deletion of any personal information about them that a business holds, with some exceptions.
- For those aged 16 and older, opt-out of personal information sales.
- Those aged 15 or younger require an opt-in for personal information sales.
- Exercise their CCPA rights without facing discrimination.

Business Obligations

To protect all consumer rights under the CCPA, compliant organizations are supposed to take several measures to meet the requirements. According to Thomson Reuters, to meet these requirements, businesses should:

- Protect personal information through appropriate security practices and procedures.
- Make all required CCPA notice disclosures, like notices when data is collected, when a privacy policy is updated, the right to opt-out of sales, etc.
- Establish processes to receive and respond to customer rights requests.
- Review all price or service of product quality differences based on collection or non-collection of information to ensure non-discriminations.
- Meet required employee training and documentation obligations.
- Review and monitor any contracts with service providers and third-party contracts to comply with the CCPA's requirements.

Enforcement

The California Attorney General (AG) is the regulatory authority for the CCPA. When a business violates the CCPA, the AG must give the business or individual in question a notice and at least 30 days to fix the issues. If the violations are not fixed within this time frame, the AG can seek penalties of up to $2500 per violation or $7500 per intentional violation.

The CCPA extends California's data breach rules by including a private right of action to consumers to seek damages for unauthorized access, theft, privacy violation, or data breach on certain personal information.

Children's Online Privacy Protection Act (COPPA)

What is COPPA?

COPPA, the Children's Online Privacy Protection Act, is a law designed to protect the privacy of children online. As more young people turn to online devices and services for daily activities, ensuring the privacy of children under thirteen has become crucial. This law establishes stringent guidelines for collecting and processing children's personal data, granting parents and guardians greater control over their children's online privacy and security.

Requirements under COPPA

COPPA sets forth several requirements to safeguard children's privacy and shield them from deceptive data collection, usage, and sharing practices. These requirements include:

- **Notification:** Websites must provide clear notifications and disclosures about the collection of information from children and the intended uses of that information.
- **Parental Consent:** Before collecting information from a child, explicit consent must be obtained from the child's parent or guardian.
- **Review Mechanisms:** Parents must be offered mechanisms and procedures to review any collected information about their child.
- **Minimal Data Collection:** Stipulations around collecting only the minimal necessary information from children.
- **Data Protection:** Establish and maintain procedures that ensure the ongoing privacy and security of the collected data.

Applicability

This law does not apply to every platform, website, or service. COPPA applies to an individual or entity if:

- They run a website or web service targeted to children under thirteen years of age and collect personal information from them or allow other entities to collect it.
- They knowingly run a plug-in, ad network, or

other services on a website targeted to children aged thirteen and under and collect personal information from them.

- Their service is directed towards a general population, but knows that children under thirteen years access it, and their personal information is collected.

Electronic Communications Privacy Act (ECPA)

What is ECPA?

The Electronic Communications Privacy Act (ECPA) is an evolution of the Federal Wiretap Act 1968. The Federal Wiretap Act originally focused on intercepting telephone conversations on traditional landlines and did not encompass online communications. ECPA was designed to bridge this gap, reflecting citizens' privacy expectations and law enforcement's legitimate needs. Today, the act covers various communications, including emails, telephone conversations, chats, and other data transmitted via the Internet.

The ECPA amalgamates three pivotal legal provisions under a single framework:

The Wiretap Act: Originating from regulations on landline telephone communications, this act makes it illegal to:

- Intentionally intercept wire, oral, or electronic communications while transmitting.

- Unlawfully use or disclose any intercepted communications.

The Stored Communications Act: safeguards both wire and electronic communications when they're not in transit (i.e. when they're "at rest"). Specifically, it's illegal to:

- Access any system used for transmitting wired or electronic communications without proper authorization.

- Alter, obtain, or prevent someone's lawful access to communications stored on such systems via unauthorized access.

The Pen Register and Trap and Trace Devices Statute regulates how the government can use "pen registers" and "trap and trace devices" to capture information about, but not the content of, wire or electronic communications.

While the laws highlighted above are among the most frequently cited in cybersecurity and privacy in the U.S., this is just an overview. Numerous other laws can apply or be exempted based on industry, geographical location, and specific circumstances. Regardless of the applicable laws, the most common way to start the compliance process is to enforce regulations, acts and standards in a local security policy approved and authorized by upper management. Leadership must implement the rules of the policy in the organization's process. This will also protect the information on critical assets.

Chapter 3: Understanding the NIST 800 RMF Framework

One of the key U.S. Cybersecurity laws, FISMA, discussed in Chapter 2, spawned the creation of security guidance from the National Institute of Standards and Technology (NIST). The guidance is published in the NIST 800 special publications. They detail the US federal government's risk-management framework (RMF). Following the NIST 800 special publications aligns the organization with cyber laws that are required for federal systems.

What is the NIST RMF Framework?

The NIST fully documents the guidance for properly managing security capabilities in the NIST 800 or NIST Risk Management Framework. To account for its wide applicability and to ensure multiple departments could benefit from the guidelines, this framework was designed in partnership with the Department of Defense (DoD), the Office of the Director of National Intelligence, and the Committee on National Security Systems. The framework emphasizes risk management by incorporating security and privacy capabilities throughout the software development life cycle (SDLC). The aim is to integrate security and privacy requirements and controls into every part of the organization, like enterprise architecture, SDLC, acquisition processes, and systems engineering processes. The framework is policy and technology-neutral and was designed with the ever-changing scope of the industry in mind. It provides a repeatable process that considers the available controls and encourages the use of automation for real-time risk management. An organization can also establish a feedback loop using precise metrics, which can help identify an efficient, cost-effective way to make decisions about the risk and best support the missions and business functions.

Purpose of the RMF

NIST identifies a few main objectives behind establishing the RMF as follows:

- The biggest objective behind having a framework is to build a security and privacy management system that aligns with an organization's mission and business objectives.
- To implement privacy, security, and response strategies that can protect individuals, information, and information systems best.
- To support informed authorization decisions and to maintain transparency in the security and privacy controls.

- To integrate security and privacy requirements into the granular level of the organization so that it becomes a natural part of every aspect of the organization.

- To promote the implementation of the Framework for Improving Critical Infrastructure Cybersecurity within federal agencies.

How to Manage Security and Privacy Risk

RMF provides guidelines on managing security and privacy risks so that organizations can mold these guidelines based on their business goals and needs. Before discussing the details of these guidelines, let's first look at some of the concepts from which these guidelines were born.

Organization-Wide Risk Management

Risk management is not an isolated process but an organization-wide undertaking. As mentioned, risk management should be addressed at every level, from mission and business planning activities to the enterprise architecture, the SDLC processes, and the systems engineering activities. It is a multi-level approach where senior leaders provide the vision and top-level goals, mid-level leaders plan, execute, and

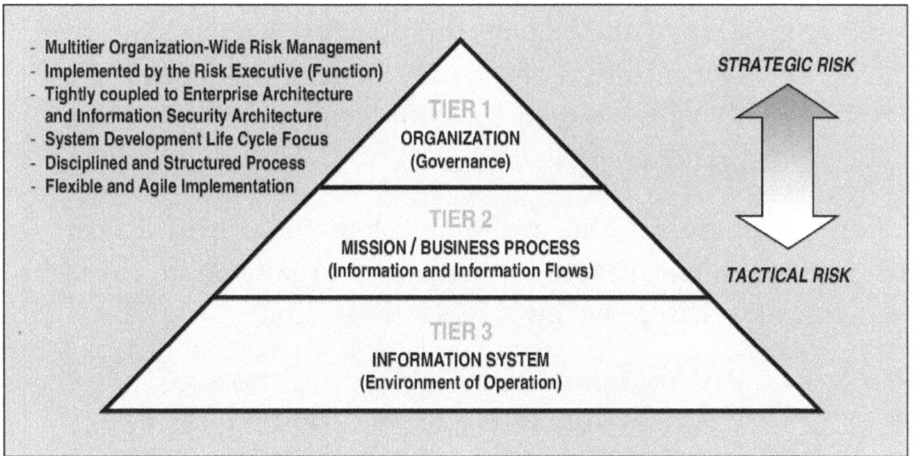

manage projects, and system-level engineers implement, operate, maintain, and iterate on projects supporting risk management within business objectives.

Organization-wide risk management can be divided into three main tiers: the organization level, the mission/business process tiers, and the information systems Tiers. An open feedback and reporting loop needs to exist in both directions to ensure that risk objectives are achieved and maintained throughout the organization.

Activities at Tiers 1 and 2 include not just managing the risk posture but understanding and planning for the integration of risk to the system level processes and must include considerations for:

- Modernization of the technologies and automation of tasks.

- The business goals and objectives.
- Optimization of the enterprise architecture.
- Resource management for maximum efficiency and cost-effectiveness.

To prepare for the proper implementation of a risk management framework within an organization, there are a few things we need to establish first:

- Risk tolerance within an organization.
- Business functions an information system is supporting.
- Key stakeholders within that information system.
- Identifying privacy and security requirements.
- Determining authorization boundaries and common access controls.

In tandem with this, organization and system-wide risk assessments should be conducted to make a risk management strategy. Based on that, threats to the systems, as well as threats to the people, need to be identified. Assets should also be identified and prioritized. Once all this information is gathered and established, we can devise a risk strategy for an information system.

Based on the decisions and strategies identified at Tier 1 and Tier 2, Tier 3 implements these decisions and controls at the ground level. Tier 3 handles the augmentation or integration of these controls, which can be common to multiple organizations/business functions or specific to the information system they are at.

The traceability of these security and privacy controls to the established requirements is also important in ensuring that identified risks are addressed at each level in the hierarchy.

RMF Steps and Structure

The NIST RMF identifies seven basic steps that must be followed for a thorough and successful risk management implementation.

1. **Prepare.** This includes all the essential activities needed for the organization to manage

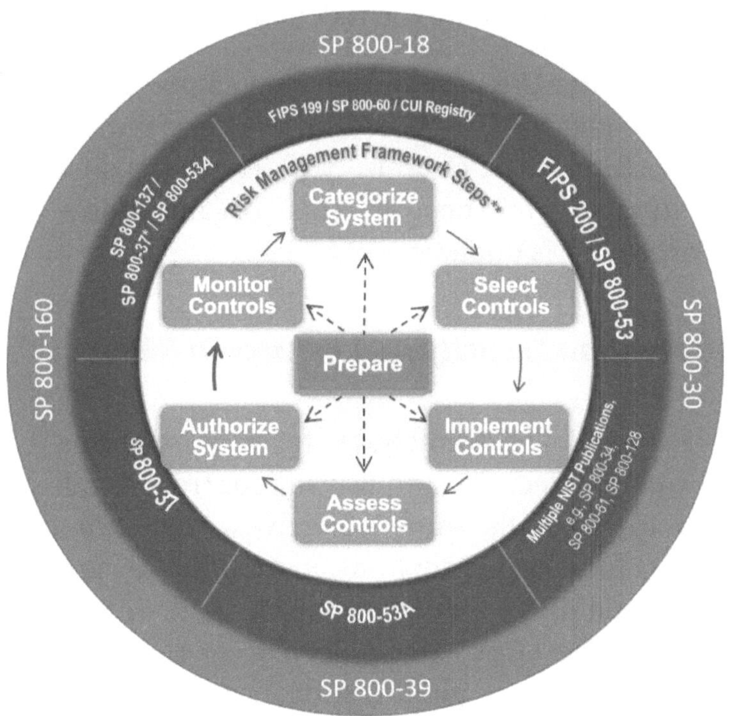

risk.

2. **Categorize.** Based on impact analysis, identify and categorize the information and systems analyzed.
3. **Select.** Select the security and privacy controls you wish to implement based on risk assessments.
4. **Implement.** Implement, deploy, and document the selected controls.
5. **Assess.** Regularly assess if the controls are relevant and working as intended.
6. Authorize. Based on the risk, authorize the systems and controls to operate within the organization.
7. **Monitor.** Continuously monitor the controls and re-evaluate the risk within the system.

All steps after the preparation step can be executed in a non-sequential way based on the requirements and risk posture of the organization. These steps can also be iterated to ensure the organization's risk management is updated.

Information Security and Privacy in RMF

RMF provides a framework for implementing both Information Security and privacy controls. While both seem to have the same objectives, they can differ. Security focuses on providing confidentiality, integrity, and availability for information and information systems. Therefore, the objective is to protect the collection, use, modification, destruction, and authorized access to data and information systems. Privacy deals with the risk of collecting, using, modifying, and deleting an individual's personally identifiable information (PII).

So whenever a system interacts with PII, it becomes key that the security and privacy controls collaborate to secure the data and protect it from unauthorized use, as well as protect the individual's privacy by disallowing access or use without the individual's consent. While these may sound extremely similar, the key here is that privacy violations can occur even with authorized system activities if the individual is not provided appropriate notice of data use and retention and the transparency of such use is not maintained.

Because of the nuanced differences in privacy and security operations, it's important to ensure collaboration of both types of controls from the very beginning to preserve both objectives during risk planning and implementation.

System and System Elements

The system elements include all parts of an information system, like the technology, the hardware, funds, and personnel, which are machine elements, human elements, and physical or environmental elements. Each element included in a system corresponds to a specific system requirement.

The authorization boundary is an important aspect of the system definition as it is key in determining which components fall within the core of an information system. This is defined during the "prepare" phase of RMF execution. An authorization boundary needs to be identified with great care and precision. If it's too broad, it can make risk management difficult, and if it's too limited, it might introduce gaps. It should include all the people, processes, and information resources directly supporting the system's business function. The scope of an authorization boundary should be revisited periodically as part of the continuous monitoring of the risk management process.

For proper RMF execution and to ensure risk is managed well, we define certain components in the entire operating environment. The system is the primary resource that needs risk management; several other factors may not fall within direct protection or authorization boundaries but interact with the system.

One of these factors is the *enabling systems*. Enabling systems are any systems that support the primary resource; they may or may not fall within the authorization boundary. They provide secondary or supporting functionalities to the system, like network services, authentication, or monitoring capabilities.

Other systems include those with which the primary resource might interact but do not directly or indirectly affect the functionalities of the primary system.

When executing RMF strategies, it can be helpful to identify the different systems interacting within a business function to better manage similar security and privacy requirements.

Requirements and Controls

Before doing any software implementation, we determine the requirements for the software. Similarly, we must know the security and privacy requirements before applying the risk management framework. These requirements include the legal and policy obligations a company must fulfill and the stakeholder requirements to protect data and systems.

When thinking about controls, we can view them as the capabilities available to fulfill a security or privacy objective or requirement. Controls interplay with requirements since they define the appropriate safeguards corresponding to the requirements.

Security and Privacy Posture

The security and privacy posture of an organization or a business function is important in determining how to approach risk management. Similarly, ongoing assessment and monitoring activities must be present even after implementing the RMF to ensure the positioning of security and privacy risk management remains optimum.

Supply-Chain Risk Management (SCRM)

Supply chain risk management comes into play

because many organizations rely on external service providers for many products and services they use to fulfill their business functions. Because of interaction with entities external to the organization, managing the risk posed by such products and services becomes important. For this, companies apply an SCRM policy, which is guided and informed by applicable laws, executive orders, directives, policies, and regulations. This policy also determines the integration of risk management between the external service and the business.

Executing the RMF

For proper execution of the NIST RMF, check out the NIST 800 Cybersecurity series by Bruce Brown and Convocourses. These books include:

- RMF ISSO: Foundations (Guide): NIST 800 Risk Management Framework for Cybersecurity Professionals (NIST 800 Cybersecurity Book 1)
- RMF ISSO: NIST 800-53 Controls: NIST 800 Control Families in Each RMF Step (NIST 800 Cybersecurity Book 2)
- RMF Security Control Assessor: NIST 800-53A Security Control Assessment Guide (NIST 800 Cybersecurity Book 3)

Chapter 4: Global Cybersecurity Laws and Regulations

Looking at the laws present only in the US gives a good idea of how important legal protection can be in providing incentives for security and privacy measures and protecting both users and organizations. This chapter will look at cyber laws worldwide to get a better context for rules and regulations designed to protect information and information systems.

Europe

Cyber Resilience Act (CRA)

The Cyber Resilience Act was created when it was realized that the cost of vulnerable hardware and software components was getting too high and needed to be addressed fundamentally. They found that products suffered from two major flaws.

1. A low level of cybersecurity by design, as seen by the number of vulnerabilities and a lack of sufficient security updates for patching new issues.
2. A lack of understanding of cybersecurity among users, which prevented them from making

choices with good security posture and/or using security measures available incorrectly or not at all

Because of this gap, the CRA was established because most of the hardware and software products were not covered by EU legislation. The aims behind this act were twofold.

The first was to encourage the manufacturers to take security and privacy seriously, creating conditions where secure products were a part of the design and development phase in a product life cycle.

The second was to create conditions for users to consider cybersecurity when choosing products with digital elements.

According to the Cyber Resilience Act - Shaping Europe's Digital Future (2022), to achieve these aims, the following four objectives were laid out as part of the CRA:

- Ensure that manufacturers improve the security of products with digital elements from the design and development phase and throughout the whole life cycle.
- Ensure a coherent cybersecurity framework, facilitating compliance for hardware and software producers.
- Enhance the transparency of security properties of products with digital elements.
- Enable businesses and consumers to use products with digital elements securely.

General Data Protection Regulation (GDPR)

What is GDPR?

General Data Protection Regulation (GDPR) is an effort to unify the data protection and privacy rules across the European Union. It went into effect in 2018 and replaced the EU Data Protection Directive 1995. GDPR aims to protect the data and individuals whose data is collected by ensuring that the companies who are collecting and storing this data are doing so in a responsible manner. It also defines the reasons for which data can be collected from individuals. The regulation says the collected data should be "limited to what is necessary in relation to the purposes for which they are processed."

Under GDPR, a person's personal information can only be processed if it meets one of the following criteria:

- The company has expressed consent to the data subject.
- Processing is necessary to perform a contract with the data subject or to take steps to enter a contract.
- Processing is necessary for compliance with a legal obligation.
- Processing is necessary to protect a data subject's or another person's vital interests.
- Processing is necessary for the performance of a task carried out in the public interest.
- Processing is necessary for legitimate interests pursued by the controller or a third party, except where the interests, rights, or freedoms of the

data subject override them.

Under GDPR, a person's name, biometric data, location, identification numbers, healthcare information, political opinions and beliefs, union memberships, or any other information that is a part of the physical, physiological, genetic, mental, economic, cultural or social identity of that person can be safeguarded.

7 Principles of GDPR

Rules of compliance of the GDPR are based on seven basic principles. These are:

1. Lawfulness, fairness, and transparency. A person collecting data must be clearly informed about how their data will be used.
2. Purpose limitation. Data can be collected only for specific purposes.
3. Data minimization. The data collected is limited to what is necessary for that specific processing.
4. Organizations collecting data must ensure its accuracy and update it as necessary. Data must be deleted or changed when the person makes such a request.
5. Storage limitation. Collected data won't be retained longer than needed.
6. Integrity and confidentiality. Appropriate protection measures must be applied to personal data to ensure it's secure and protected against theft or unauthorized use.
7. Entities collecting personal data are responsible

for ensuring compliance with the GDPR.

These seven principles are based on each individual's specific rights under GDPR.

- Right to be forgotten. All individuals can ask for their PII to be erased from an organization's database.
- Right of access. Individuals can always access and review the data they have provided to an organization.
- Right to object. An individual can always refuse permission to provide any personal data.
- Right to rectification. Individuals can ask for inaccurate personal information to be corrected.
- Right of portability. An individual may at all times view and transfer their personal information.

Who Does It Apply To?

All organizations collecting, storing, processing, or sharing any personal information of an EU member citizen are required to comply with GDPR. The organization may or may not reside within the EU but should be in compliance if they are collecting data from the citizens of a member nation.

In case of a breach, the organization is required to notify the supervisory authority within 72 hours of the breach. If this notification isn't made within 72 hours, the organization must provide a justifiable reason for the delay. The breach notification must include at least the nature of the breach, the number and types of data subjects' data that could be compromised, and the number of data records that could be involved. All breach victims must also be informed individually about the potential loss or data leak, not as a general announcement.

Best Practices

Some of the best practices to follow to ensure GDPR compliance are:

- Proper disclosure before collecting any information.
- Collecting only that which is required, since whether an organization uses some data or not, they will be responsible for all the collected data.
- All data, while stored and transmitted, must be encrypted to ensure confidentiality.
- Ensure that there are at least two backups of the data at two separate off-site locations, which are kept up-to-date.
- Provide individuals with the option to modify and erase the personal data they have provided.

Japan

Act on the Protection of Personal Information (APPI)

What is APPI?

APPI, or the Act on the Protection of Personal

Information, stands as a beacon of data protection in Japan, marking the nation's commitment to safeguarding personal information. This pioneering legislation was not only one of the first privacy laws to be established in Asia but also holds the distinction of being the first law to receive an adequacy decision from the EU post the inception of the GDPR.

Administered and upheld by the Personal Information Protection Committee (PPC), the APPI sets itself apart with a dedicated stipulation mandating reviews and updates every three years. This ensures its provisions remain relevant and robust in the ever-evolving data protection landscape.

The law casts a wide net, applying to all business operators—both within and outside of Japan—that handle personal data from individuals in Japan. However, government organizations and other administrative entities under distinct regulations enjoy exemption from the APPI.

The APPI categorizes personal data into two distinct types: "personal information" and "special care-required personal information." The former encompasses typical PII, such as names, addresses, dates of birth, email addresses, biometric data, and other unique identifiers like driver's license or passport numbers.

On the other hand, "special care-required" personal information covers data that has potential discriminatory implications. This includes, but is not limited to, medical histories, marital status, race, religious beliefs, and criminal records.

With its rigorous guidelines and stipulations, the APPI stands as a testament to Japan's dedication to safeguarding individual privacy rights, striking a balance between the increasing utility of personal information in advanced societies and the rights and interests of individuals.

Rights and Responsibilities
Users' Rights:

The Act on the Protection of Personal Information (APPI) empowers individuals with several rights regarding their data:

- **Disclosure Request:** Users can inquire how their data is stored, processed, and shared.
- **Complaint Mechanism:** They have a right to clear information on where to submit complaints related to data usage and handling.
- **Data Erasure or Limited Use:** Individuals can request either deleting their data or limiting its usage to specific operations.
- **Legal Recourse:** If business operators don't provide the requested information within two weeks, users can initiate legal action against them.
- **Data Retention Period:** The aforementioned rights are applicable irrespective of the data storage duration, whether short-term or long-

term.

Business Operators' Responsibilities:

To comply with APPI, business operators are expected to:

- Privacy Policy: Establish a privacy policy clearly articulating the reasons for data collection.
- Data Security: Implement robust privacy and security measures to safeguard the collected personal data.
- User Request Procedure: Set up and maintain procedures to handle user requests related to data disclosure and handling.
- Data Breach Notification: Post the 2020 amendment, in the event of a data breach, businesses are obligated to inform both the PPC and the affected users promptly.

Data Transfers

Before the 2020 amendments, APPI did not mandate businesses to notify users when sharing their data with third-party vendors unless the user had actively chosen to opt out after being informed. This oversight allowed for potentially unauthorized data sharing with other entities.

However, the 2020 amendment addressed and rectified this gap. Businesses must obtain clear and explicit user consent before transferring their data to third-party organizations. Exceptions exist for matters of public interest, such as legal proceedings or national security, where prior consent is deemed unnecessary.

For international data transfers, APPI stipulates that businesses should ensure that recipient countries or companies adhere to data protection standards that are on par with those upheld in Japan.

Penalties Under the 2020 APPI Amendments:

The amendments made to APPI in 2020 introduced stringent penalties for non-compliance:

Organizations: Businesses or entities found violating the provisions of APPI can now be levied with significant fines. The ceiling for these financial penalties has been set at ¥100 million, which translates to approximately USD 815,000.

Individuals: On a personal level, individuals involved in breaches of the APPI can face severe repercussions. They might be subjected to incarceration for durations extending up to a year. Alternatively, they can be slapped with monetary penalties, going as high as ¥1 million - approximately USD 8,150.

False Reporting: The amendments also emphasize the reporting process's integrity. Individuals or entities found guilty of submitting fabricated or misleading reports to the Personal Information Protection Committee (PPC) can incur fines up to ¥500,000, equivalent to around USD 4,000.

These revamped penalties underscore the seriousness with which Japan regards data protection, ensuring that businesses and individuals think twice before engaging in any malpractices related to personal data.

China

Cyber Security Law

The Cybersecurity Law, enacted in 2017 by the People's Republic of China, provides comprehensive measures to protect data, ensure data localization, and fortify national cybersecurity. As Wagner (2017) highlights, this law mandates certain network operators to store specific data domestically and permits Chinese authorities to conduct ad-hoc reviews of a company's network operations. While the exact stipulations of the law are often perceived as somewhat ambiguous, several key provisions warrant attention:

Article 28: This law section stipulates that "network operators" — a term broadly interpreted to encompass social media platforms, application developers, and other tech entities — must cooperate with public security agencies such as the Ministry of Public Security. They are obligated to provide requested information when called upon.

Article 35: This article primarily focuses on acquiring foreign software or hardware by government bodies or "critical information infrastructure operators." It mandates that any such purchased hardware or software be vetted by Chinese agencies, including entities like China's State Cryptography Administration.

Article 37: Central to the theme of data localization, this provision dictates that foreign tech companies functioning in the Chinese landscape must house data related to Chinese users within servers located on the Chinese mainland.

Information Security Technology – Personal Information Security Specification

What is the Specification?

This data protection specification came into effect in 2018. Although not a mandatory regulation, it represents a significant advancement in the context of China's Cyber Security Law. Given the increasing global focus on privacy considerations, this specification merits individual discussion. Analogous to APPI, it categorizes personal information into two types:

Sensitive Personal Information: This category encompasses data whose disclosure could jeopardize a person's safety or lead to prejudice or discrimination. This type of data includes ID card numbers, biological identifiers, bank account details, religious beliefs, and sexual orientation, among others.

General Personal Information: This type typically covers data such as names, dates of birth, and the like.

Data Collection Requirements: The specification outlines requirements to ensure the justified collection and usage of individual data:

- **Minimization Principle:** This principle emphasizes that only information directly relevant to the business's objective should be collected and stored. Superfluous data collection should be strictly avoided.
- **Prior Consent:** Individuals must be informed before collecting data, and their explicit consent should be secured.

Exceptions to Mandatory Consent: Certain circumstances may bypass the general consent rule. As delineated by Norton Rose Fulbright in January 2018, these exceptions come into play when:

- Collecting personal information pertains directly to national security, public interest, or judicial processes.
- Collecting personal information is essential to protect specific individuals' personal interests, property rights, or other crucial legal interests, especially when obtaining consent is impracticable.
- The data stems from publicly disclosed information by the individual or legitimate public news sources.
- Personal data collection serves the intent of forming and executing a contract per an individual's request.
- Collecting personal data is vital for maintaining a product or service, such as software bug resolution.
- Personal data collection serves the purpose of legitimate news reporting.
- Personal data collection aids academic research, provided the data is anonymized before publication.
- Any other scenarios defined by existing laws and regulations.

Singapore

Cybersecurity Act

The Cybersecurity Act stands as Singapore's primary legislation for cybersecurity matters. It is designed to establish a robust legislative framework for protecting Critical Information Infrastructure (CII) and to empower the Cybersecurity Agency of Singapore (CSA) with the authority to address cybersecurity incidents within Singapore.

A computer or system qualifies as a CII if:

- It provides essential services, the disruption of which could significantly impede the normal operation of these services.
- It exists either entirely or partially within Singapore.

The "Cybersecurity Code of Practice for Critical Information Infrastructure" (often referred to as the Cybersecurity Code) has been instituted to supplement this act. This code specifies the standard practices that CII owners are expected to adhere to. As stipulated by the Cybersecurity Code:

- CII owners are mandated to establish, implement, and continually uphold a cybersecurity risk management framework.
- They must also have a cybersecurity incident

response plan in place, coupled with a crisis communication strategy.
- Moreover, developing a Business Continuity Plan (BCP) and a Disaster Recovery Plan (DRP) is essential for CII owners.

Singapore's Cybersecurity Act serves as the nation's primary cybersecurity legislation. The core purpose of this law is to establish a robust legislative framework for safeguarding Critical Information Infrastructure (CII) and bestowing upon the Cybersecurity Agency of Singapore (CSA) the mandate to manage cybersecurity incidents within the country. A system is designated as CII if:

It's a computer or information system that delivers essential services, where any disruption could critically affect the regular operation of these services.

This system is located either entirely or partially within Singapore.

The "Cybersecurity Code of Practice for Critical Information Infrastructure" (often called the Cybersecurity Code) was rolled out in tandem with this act. This code delineates the benchmark practices CII owners should adhere to. According to the Cybersecurity Code:

- CII owners must establish, implement, and persistently uphold a cybersecurity risk management framework.
- They must also maintain a cybersecurity incident response plan and a crisis

communication strategy.

- Furthermore, CII owners must formulate a Business Continuity Plan (BCP) and a Disaster Recovery Plan (DRP).

Personal Data Protection Act (PDPA)

The PDPA addresses the protection and privacy of personal data, not limited to online environments. It often complements other industry-specific laws by enhancing them. Under the PDPA, organizations are bound by specific obligations related to data collection and storage, and it also emphasizes an individual's rights over their data.

Obligations for Data Collection:

- Notification Obligation: Organizations must inform individuals about their data's intended collection and use.
- Consent Obligation: Organizations must obtain clear consent from individuals before collecting their data.
- Purpose Limitation Obligation: Organizations can only collect personal data that is necessary and relevant for a legitimate purpose.

Obligations for Data Storage and Maintenance:

- Accuracy Obligation: Organizations must ensure the accuracy of their personal data.
- Protection Obligation: Organizations must implement security measures to protect

personal data from unauthorized access or leaks.

- Retention Limitation Obligation: Personal data should be deleted or anonymized once it's no longer needed for the purpose for which it was collected.
- Transfer Limitation Obligation: Personal data can only be transferred to a country or territory if it offers a comparable standard of data protection as the PDPA.

Individual's Rights Over Personal Data:

- Access and Correction: Individuals have the right to access and correct their data held by organizations.
- Breach Notification: In the event of a data breach, organizations must notify affected individuals about the breach and its potential impact.
- Data Portability Obligation: Upon request, organizations must transfer an individual's data to another organization of the individual's choosing, subject to certain conditions.

India

Information Technology (IT) Act

The IT Act is the foundational legislation addressing most privacy and security regulations for entities operating within India. This Act draws inspiration from the United Nations Model Law on Electronic Commerce 1996 (UNCITRAL Model). According to the IT Act, if the source of an offense, such as the computer or device utilized, is situated in India, then the perpetrator can be prosecuted under the provisions of this Act.

Objectives of the IT Act:

- To safeguard transactions conducted electronically.
- To offer legal validity to electronic communications and exchanges.
- To authenticate digital signatures used for legal purposes.
- To monitor and regulate the activities of digital intermediaries, ensuring they operate within legal bounds.
- To ensure the privacy of citizens' data.
- To govern and secure sensitive data on social media platforms and other electronic intermediaries.
- To officially recognize books of accounts

maintained electronically per the standards set by the Reserve Bank of India Act, 1934.

Penalties under the IT Act:

An offender who, without the rightful owner's permission, causes damage to a computer or system is liable to compensate for the harm inflicted. Additionally, penalties can be imposed on individuals who:

- Unlawfully download, copy, or access data from a system.
- Introduce malicious software or viruses to a computer system.
- Cause disruptions in the functioning of the system.
- Deny system access to the rightful owner or authorized personnel.
- Tamper with, alter, or manipulate the system.
- Illegally delete, modify, or alter data stored in the system.
- Steal or unlawfully retrieve information from the system.

It's worth noting that while the discussed regulations provide a general framework, several other data privacy and security laws are operational in different nations, each with its unique stipulations. The laws mentioned here are among the most widely applicable and enforced. However, they possess intricacies not covered in this brief overview. To ensure complete compliance with any given law, it's crucial to undertake a comprehensive review of its provisions and conduct periodic assessments.

73

Chapter 5: Industry-Specific Cybersecurity Laws and Regulations

In this chapter, we delve into industry-specific cyber laws and regulations. Each industry, with its unique set of challenges and vulnerabilities, has tailored cyber laws and regulations to mitigate risks and enhance security postures. The harmonization and enforcement of these laws across various sectors are paramount to fostering a safe, secure, and resilient cyberspace. In this chapter, we will explore the specific laws, their implementations, compliance challenges, and the ramifications for non-compliance, offering readers insights into the multifaceted world of industry-specific cyber regulations.

- **Health Care:** The health care industry has acts and laws to guard sensitive patient health records and ensure the privacy of medical data.
- **Retail:** Retail stores have protections for consumer details and transaction records to maintain the integrity of online commerce.
- **Financial:** Banks and financial institutions have laws that ensure the security of financial transactions, user banking details, and other proprietary financial information.

- **Government & Defense:** Federal and state governments are subject to laws that safeguard national data and citizen records and ensure the resilience of critical infrastructure.
- **Manufacturing:** For manufacturers, some regulations protect intellectual properties, ensure safe and secure automated systems, and guard trade secrets.
- **IT Services:** Information technology companies must adhere to laws and regulations safeguarding digital infrastructure. These regulations protect data during the transit and storage of client data and ensure robustness against cyber threats.
- **Hospitality**: The hospitality industry consists of other sectors like tourism, theme parks, bars, hotels, and restaurants (just to name a few). Organizations in the hospitality industry need to protect the information of guests. They must also protect reservation systems and payment details while ensuring privacy and security in an increasingly digital hospitality sector.
- **Pharmaceuticals (Pharma):** The pharma sector has special protections that overlap with other industries, such as health care. This sector has laws designed to protect drug research data and patient trial information and maintain the confidentiality of proprietary formulas.

There are countless sectors, industries, and niches

shaped by cybersecurity law. We will spotlight a few to offer an understanding of how these regulations span various industries. This chapter will cover health care, retail, and finance. Government and Defense will be covered in the next chapter.

The necessity for such tailored laws arises from the unique nature of the data each industry manages. Beyond just personal identifiable information (PII), these sectors deal with data—ranging from health records to proprietary drug formulations—that could have significant implications if mishandled or breached. In the following sections, we'll provide an overview of some of the most influential cybersecurity laws in the U.S. While our discussion aims to be informative, it's essential to note that this is not an exhaustive catalog. Specific laws might vary in relevance depending on the industry under consideration and their location.

HealthCare

Healthcare has emerged as one of the most important industries regarding data privacy and security. A patient's health data is important and can differentiate between life and death. For this, there need to be special requirements on how this data is collected and handled at all times.

Health Insurance Portability and Accountability Act (HIPAA)

What is HIPAA?

HIPAA stands for the Health Insurance Portability and Accountability Act. It is a federal privacy and security regulation that applies to the healthcare industry in general. All healthcare corporations and organizations handling healthcare information are required to be compliant with HIPAA to be able to operate in the US. It has been designed to protect a patient's sensitive information and prevent its disclosure without their knowledge and consent. With the rising health insurance costs, it was developed with the idea that a patient may be able to carry forward their health insurance even after losing their jobs. To protect them from discrimination because of pre-existing health conditions and to guarantee coverage renewability with a new employer. To provide all this, the law was divided into two parts: the privacy rule and the security rule.

The Privacy Rule

The privacy rule primarily deals with maintaining the privacy of a patient's protected health information (PHI). The rule invokes duality because, for effective treatment, the PHI needs to be shared and transferred to the relevant healthcare providers. Still, at the same time, the patients have the right for their medical and PII to remain confidential.

For this, the Minimum Necessary Standard is applied, according to which the healthcare providers can access the information they need to do their job but nothing beyond that. Any other disclosures of a patient's information cannot happen without their consent except when it is required by law, to another covered entity, or if the disclosure is in the patient's or public's interest.

Another mandate is that the patient can always access and review their own data and request modifications and restrictions over their data.

The Security Rule

The security rule applies to healthcare corporations in that they must maintain the necessary safeguards over PHI to maintain the privacy and security of the data. This should include administrative, physical, and technical measures. According to Josh Fruhlinger (CSO Online, Jan 2021), the overall goals are:

- Ensure the confidentiality, integrity, and availability of all PHI handled or transmitted.
- Protect against reasonably anticipated threats to the security or integrity of the information.
- Protect against reasonably anticipated but impermissible uses or disclosures.
- Ensure workplace compliance.

That said, the rule does not mandate how these measures should be taken, and corporations can determine how best to implement these practices based on their unique needs.

Covered Entities

According to the Centres for Disease Control and Prevention, The following entities are covered under HIPAA:

- Healthcare providers: Every healthcare provider, regardless of the practice size, electronically transmits health information in connection with certain transactions.
- Health plans: All health plans, including health, dental, vision, and prescription drug insurers; Health maintenance organizations (HMOs), Medicare, Medicaid, Medicare+Choice, and Medicare supplement insurers; long-term care insurers, employer-sponsored group health plans, government- and church-sponsored health plans.
- Healthcare clearinghouses: Service providers receive and process non-standard information to standard values and formats.
- Business associates: These people provide other services to covered entities that involve using PHI, like claims processing, billing, etc.

Uses and Disclosures

The law permits the use or disclosure of PHI without a patient's authorization only under the following situations:

- Disclosure to the individual
- For treatment, operations, and payments

- Incident to an otherwise permitted use or disclosure
- Limited dataset for research, public health, or healthcare operations
- Public interest and benefit activities

Health Information Trust (HITRUST) Common Security Framework (CSF)

Even though it's not a law, we will quickly mention HITRUST since it is a framework often used to help healthcare organizations comply with cyber law. The Health Information Trust (HITRUST) Alliance originally created the HITRUST Common Security Framework to encompass HIPAA and other healthcare laws. The HITRUST Alliance wanted a framework that, when implemented, would cover these laws, and a company then did not have to do a lot of extra work to maintain compliance with all the laws. Since then, It has expanded to include laws like PCI-DSS, GDPR, and others to create a unified framework. Under HITRUST, there are a set of policies and procedures to improve the cyber security strategies of an organization to bring them in compliance with the laws. Because it unifies so many laws, HITRUST would suggest different policies and procedures to different organizations based on the laws they must comply with.

What is the certification?

The HITRUST CSF certification is not government-mandated. In the case of external audits, showing a HITRUST certification does not directly imply compliance with a certain law; proof of all the different policy compliance must be provided. However, because the framework consists of policies for all the different laws, having a HITRUST certification means that no extra effort is needed to pass audits and meet compliance requirements for a law. Because of this, it has become standard industry practice to have this certification. It can be especially useful for service providers and third-party organizations who don't directly fall under a specific law but process some data or provide a service requiring compliance. A HITRUST certification can assure other organizations that all required practices are being followed. For this reason, many contracts now include a HITRUST certification requirement.

HITRUST Requirements

The specific means and ways for following a control defined within the objectives are called requirements. Based on an organization's size and business functions, these requirements and implementations can look very different from one organization to the other. For this, the requirement levels are defined. They are tailored based on different organizations' type, size, and capacities.

Josh Fruhlinger (CSO Online, May 2021) describes that the process of becoming HITRUST certified begins with a detailed institutional self-assessment. This questionnaire asks about your organization's size, risk exposure, and other factors. The answers to this questionnaire will determine which controls, requirements, and levels you'll need to implement.

Retail

Companies like Walmart, Target, and TJMax rely heavily on consumers to buy retail products. They may have other services that dabble in health care or other sectors. Still, most of their business and infrastructure are dedicated to buying or creating bulk manufactured products and selling them at a marked-up retail price. These organizations are in the retail sector. Their supply chain, logistics, and technical infrastructure give them unique cybersecurity challenges that require specific solutions and laws.

The main way that these institutions collect money is point of sale (POS) devices. The old name for these systems is "cash registers." These POS systems have evolved to take digital transactions. Most transactions in the developed world are done with credit, debit, or phone transactions, which can be an easy target for criminal hackers. The response to the increase in digital transactions was laws to protect them.

Payment Card Industry Data Security Standard (PCI-DSS)

What is PCI-DSS?

This law is primarily designed to protect the payment card industry from fraud and improve data security within the industry. Any organization that accepts, stores, processes, or transfers payment card data, like debit or credit cards, must comply with PCI-DSS. It's not mandated by federal law but by the Payment Card Industry Security Standards Council, which comprises major credit card companies and has been included in many state laws.

Who Needs to Comply?

PCI-DSS primarily applies to:

- Merchants. Even if all the PCI-DSS activities are outsourced, as a seller online, they are responsible for all contracted parties being compliant.
- Service providers. If they receive, store, process, or transmit cardholder information or can affect the security of cardholder data in any way, they are required to comply.

The Twelve Requirements

There are twelve requirements that every compliant organization must meet:

1. Installing and maintaining a firewall. Since firewalls provide network monitoring and protection, they are useful to protect data during transmission.
2. Updating the vendor-supplied defaults for system passwords and security parameters. Defaults can be weak, exposed, or otherwise redundantly used.
3. Protecting stored data. Protecting cardholder data at rest by encrypting it, restricting access, using secure storage facilities, and destroying data timely.
4. Encrypting data during transmission. Especially when transferring over open or public networks, data should be encrypted.
5. Updating security software. Keep all anti-virus and other security software up to date and apply all security patches on time.
6. Developing and maintaining secure systems. Organizations can develop inherently secure systems and software by introducing security into their SDLC.
7. Restricting access. Access to cardholder data should be restricted to the employees on a need-to-know basis.
8. Uniquely identifying each person with access. Assigning them a unique ID so that their activities can be appropriately monitored.
9. Restricting physical access to data. All the devices storing or processing cardholder data should have restricted access.

10. Tracking and monitoring all network activities. To ensure sensitive cardholder information is not being accessed without authorization or requirement.
11. Putting a security policy in place for all employees and contractors.
12. Regularly Testing Security Systems and Processes: Implement a robust testing schedule to regularly check security systems, including firewalls, antivirus, and encryption protocols, to ensure they are functioning optimally.

Penalties

The penalties for non-compliance can be monetary and non-monetary. Non-monetary losses can include loss of customer confidence, loss of business and jobs, diminishing sales, termination of the ability to accept payment cards, etc. Whereas monetary losses include legal costs, settlements, fines, penalties, cost of reissuing payment cards, higher subsequent cost of compliance, etc.

Financial Sector

Because of the complexity of the stock market and trading, companies are more likely to skirt ethical practices. There are more chances for an individual's data to be lost, exposed, or misused when dealing with publicly traded companies. For this, the Sarbanes-Oxley Act was created.

Sarbanes-Oxley (SOX) Act

What is SOX?

The SOX Act, drafted by congressmen Paul Sarbanes and Michael Oxley, was passed by the US Congress to protect individual investors from fraudulent and unethical practices by corporations. Tunggal (2022) states, "The legislation set new and expanded requirements for all U.S. public company boards, management, and public accounting firms to increase transparency in financial reporting and formalizing systems for internal controls."

This means that a public company must individually certify the accuracy of a financial statement. The legislation also increased the independence of the external reviewers of financial reporting and increased the responsibilities of the board of directors with respect to the correctness of reporting. There are mandates to limit access to this data as well, which, as a side benefit, also increases the security and privacy of the sensitive data.

Five Pillars of Data Security

SOX data security frameworks have five fundamentals to follow:

1. Ensuring the security of financial data.
2. Preventing unauthorized access and tampering with data.
3. Tracking breach attempts and documenting and implementing remediation measures.

4. Monitoring data access and other controls and having logs available for auditors.
5. Demonstrating compliance on an ongoing basis.

Who Should Comply?

The following types of organizations must comply with SOX:

- All publicly traded companies, wholly-owned subsidiaries, foreign companies that are publicly traded and do business in the United States, and even accounting firms that audit public companies.
- Private companies planning their Initial Public Offering (IPO) must comply with SOX before going public.

Private companies, charities, and non-profits generally do not need to comply, but they can have penalties imposed for knowingly destroying or falsifying financial information.

There are some more stipulations for the organizations which are required to comply. Firms that audit a company's books cannot be involved in any other business function for the said company, including business valuations, designing and implementing information systems, etc. Whistleblower protection is available where a company cannot retaliate against someone potentially reporting a federal offense. Payroll system controls must be established, and the company's workforce, salaries, benefits, incentives, paid time off, and training costs must be accounted for.

Requirements for SOX

To comply with SOX regulations, organizations must conduct yearly audits that account for the integrity of all data processes and financial statements and ensure adequate data security. Some of the most important requirements are discussed below:

- Section 302. Section 302 states that the Chief Executive Officer (CEO) and Chief Financial Officer (CFO) are responsible for the accuracy, documentation, and submission of all financial reports and the internal control structure to the SEC.
- Section 404. It requires that all annual financial reports include an Internal Control Report where the management takes responsibility for internal controls and an assessment of said controls to ensure they are adequate.
- Section 409. Accordingly, any material changes in the financial conditions or operations must be reported in real-time.
- Section 802. This imposes penalties of up to 20 years imprisonment for falsifying financial statements or tampering with legal investigations.
- Section 806. It protects against retaliation by whistleblowers against a company.

Penalties

Penalties for non-compliance with SOX include but are

not limited to fines, removal and delisting from public stock exchanges, and invalidation of D&O insurance policies.

Chapter 6: Cybersecurity Laws in Government and Defense

Similar to healthcare and payment card industries, the federal government has rules that pertain to it. Certain government organizations have to follow special regulations because of the kind of data they receive and work with. Any contractor, service provider, or third-party organization working with these government bodies must also adhere to the same or similar standards to maintain data security and privacy of citizens' data. The National Aeronautics and Space Administration (NASA) and the Department of Defense (DoD) are two such entities that require special data handling procedures and are discussed in this chapter.

NASA Cyber Security Policies

NASA has its cybersecurity policy and procedures as defined by the office of the Chief Information Security Officer. The main policy is called the NASA Policy Directive (NPD) 2810.

What is NPD 2810?

The NPD 2810 is a policy directive defining the policies protecting classified and unclassified information within NASA. Since the threat of cyber attacks on NASA systems and networks is higher, they must take additional protection measures.

According to the NPD 2810.1F - Main (2022), the following policies apply:

- Secure all NASA information and information systems, both classified and unclassified, in a manner commensurate with their national security classification level, sensitivity, value, and criticality.
- Fully implement the guidance in the NIST SP 800 series on computer security policies, procedures, and guidelines, and the NIST Federal Information Processing Standards (FIPS) as directed in Office of Management and Budget Circular A-130, "Managing Information as a Strategic Resource" and the Federal Information Security Modernization Act (FISMA) of 2014.
- Incorporate information security throughout the entire system life cycle to protect NASA information and information systems.
- Manage the cybersecurity of all classified and unclassified information systems acquired, developed, or used to support NASA missions, programs, projects, and institutional partnerships through the complete system life cycle.

- Establish and manage sound risk management and cybersecurity processes.
- Conduct continuous monitoring and reviews of NASA information systems to verify compliance with applicable Federal laws and NASA policies.
- Investigate information security incidents and develop after-action reports following significant incidents to address issues and improve future responses.
- Ensure information security policy requirements, audits, and forensic investigations are implemented and coordinated across Centers and contracts.
- Implement applicable cybersecurity policy best practices and guidance.
- Ensure that software developed to support NASA missions, programs, and projects and used on NASA information systems is secure.
- Ensure all information systems, classified and unclassified, operating within the NASA environment operate under valid authorization from an Authorizing Official per the Assessment and Authorization process.

Applicability

The NASA cybersecurity policy applies to:

- NASA Headquarters and NASA Centers, including Component Facilities and Technical and Service Support Centers.

- The Jet Propulsion Laboratory (JPL), a Federally Funded Research and Development Center, other contractors, grant recipients, or parties to agreements only to the extent specified or referenced in the contracts, grants, or agreements.
- All NASA users of information systems (e.g., civil servants and contractors) when supporting Agency projects, programs, and missions.

Responsibilities

Primarily, the responsibility is shared between the Office of the Chief Information Officer (OCIO), responsible for protecting unclassified information, and the Office of Protective Services (OPS), responsible for protecting classified information. However, the NPD 2810 further expands on the other key stakeholder responsibilities with respect to the cybersecurity policy.

The NASA Administrator

An example of NASA roles and responsibilities is the NASA administrator. According to the NPD 2810, they do the following:

- Provides information security protections commensurate with the risk and magnitude of the harm resulting from unauthorized access, use, disclosure, disruption, modification, or destruction of information collected or maintained by or on behalf of NASA or within information systems used or operated by NASA, by a NASA contractor, or another organization on behalf of NASA.

- Ensures Agency information systems comply with FISMA and other Federal laws, related policies, procedures, standards, and guidelines on unclassified information security and national security systems (i.e., classified systems).
- Ensures that information security management processes are integrated with NASA's strategic and operational planning processes.
- Ensures that senior NASA officials provide information security for the information and information systems that support the operations and assets under their control with the help of proper risk assessments to determine the level of security controls, provide the required resources, and implement and monitor the procedures.

NASA and other federal organizations use internal policies such as NPD 2810 to comply with laws and regulations. The policy is implemented through procedures and processes for all employees and contractors working with federally controlled data.

DoD Security Requirements

The Department of Defense (DoD) has to follow several security rules and regulations regarding the kind of data and information they have available to them. Contractors, service providers, and third-party organizations working with DoD must follow the same regulations. Previous chapters have discussed the NIST 800 risk management framework security standards. In this chapter, we will introduce others mandated by federal laws.

Defense Federal Acquisition Regulation Supplement (DFARS)

What is DFARS?

Defense Federal Acquisition Regulation Supplement (DFARS) was implemented in 2015 after the Executive Order (EO) 2010 was deemed incomplete to protect Controlled Unclassified Information (CUI). The primary purpose behind DFARS was for the DoD and allied organizations to be able to protect the confidentiality of that information, which is sensitive and in the interest of the US but not strictly regulated by the federal government. The NIST 800-171 is a big part of DFARS and is discussed separately in the next section.

Who must Comply?

Anyone contracted by the DoD with access to CUI must comply with DFARS. Larger or smaller defense contractors or potential contractors looking to get defense contracts must all comply with DFARS to be eligible to work with the DoD.

Requirements

The minimum requirement for DFARS is that any CUI that resides in or moves through an organization's information system must be protected by adequate security measures.

Contractors and non-federal organizations must conduct a readiness assessment and provide objective proof that addresses all these requirements before becoming DFARS compliant. The categories of DFARS requirements are as follows:

- Access Control
- Awareness and Training
- Audit and Accountability
- Configuration Management
- Identification and Authentication
- Incident Response
- Maintenance
- Media Protection
- Personnel Security
- Physical Protection
- Risk Assessment
- Security Assessment
- System and Communications Protection
- System and Information Integrity

NIST SP 800-171

What is NIST 800-171?

NIST 800-171 is a set of cybersecurity standards that must be adhered to by organizations that process or store Controlled Unclassified Information (CUI) on behalf of the US government. Such organizations might include Department of Defense contractors, universities and research institutions that receive federal grants, and entities offering services to government agencies. To ensure compliance with NIST 800-171, organizations handling CUI must perform self-assessments to ascertain and maintain this compliance.

This framework is distinct from NIST 800-37, a risk management framework. While NIST 800-37 primarily focuses on federally owned systems that process federal data, usually within federal facilities, and can range from unclassified to classified data, NIST 800-171 specifically addresses supporting organizations collaborating with the Department of Defense. All NIST 800 standards are based on FISMA.

Requirements

There are about 110 requirements under the NIST 800-171, divided into 14 families.

1. Access Control. This family of requirements deals with access to networks, systems, and information. These also determine the flow of information within the system and who can and

cannot access certain information.

2. Awareness and Training. This includes ensuring system administrators and users know security risks and related cybersecurity procedures and that employees are trained to perform security-related roles.

3. Audit and Accountability. This focuses on auditing and analyzing system and event logs, the best practices for analyzing the logs, and reporting on data.

4. Configuration Management. This includes ensuring the proper configuration of hardware, software, and devices across the organization's system and network. It also provides restrictions for unauthorized software downloads and installs.

5. Identification and Authentication. This family of requirements ensures that only authenticated users can access the organization's network or systems.

6. Incident Response. This family is responsible for ensuring proper plans and procedures are in place to deal with possible security incidents.

7. Maintenance. This family provides insight into best practices for systems and network maintenance procedures.

8. Media Protection. These requirements cover best practices for storing and destroying sensitive information and media in physical and digital formats.

9. Personnel Security. This deals with ensuring that the personnel accessing the secure information are screened for security and also manages the cleaning up of data and access after

the termination of personnel or contracts.

10. Physical Protection. This includes physically protecting all the hardware, devices, and equipment an information system uses.
11. Risk Assessment. Under this family, organizations are required to conduct regular assessments of their systems and devices, analyze them for vulnerabilities, and maintain their security posture.
12. Security Assessment. This is specifically to ensure the procedures and plans used for security are working as expected and achieving the security objectives they are designed for.
13. System and Communications Protection. This family mainly focuses on protecting data in transit, ensuring secure network communications, and only allowing authorized transfers.
14. System and Information Integrity. This deals with the ongoing protection and maintenance of all the systems in an organization.

Who Should Comply?

Although 800-171 applies to all organizations dealing with CUI. In particular, some of the common types of organizations that need to comply are:

- Defense contractors
- Organizations providing financial services
- Web and communication service providers
- Healthcare data processors

- Systems Integrators
- Colleges and universities that utilize federal data or information
- Research institutes and labs receiving federal grants and information

Best Practices

Because the NIST 800-171 compliance relies on self-assessments, some of the standard best practices to follow for executing a self-assessment are:

- Form an assessment team with input from senior information security stakeholders.
- Set an assessment plan, including a time frame and objectives.
- Begin an internal communication campaign to spread awareness of the project.
- Create a contact list of personnel with relevant responsibilities, such as system administrators and information security specialists.
- Collect relevant documents, including existing security policies, system records and manuals, previous audit results and logs, admin guidance, and system architecture documents.
- Assess individual requirements in the NIST 800-171 document and record a statement for each.
- Create an action plan outlining how any unmet requirements will be achieved.
- Include all evidence for compliance in a System Security Plan (SSP) document.

Cybersecurity Maturity Model Certification (CMMC)

What is CMMC?

Cybersecurity Maturity Model Certification (CMMC) is an amalgamation of the above DFARS and NIST 800-171 regulations and additional rules to create a unified national standard for cybersecurity. It was created by the Office of the Under Secretary of Defense (OUSD) for Acquisition & Sustainment. It seeks to respond to cyber threats by standardizing how DoD contractors secure critical information. The biggest difference between NIST 800-171 and CMMC is that while NIST 800-171 allows organizations to self-assess their cybersecurity compliance, CMMC requires third-party assessments to ensure that contractors meet certain cybersecurity standards before they can be awarded contracts.

This shift to third-party assessment aims to provide higher assurance that contractors are adequately protecting sensitive data, and it introduces five levels of certification, each with a set of supporting practices and processes. While NIST 800-171 has requirements that organizations must meet, CMMC expands upon those requirements and adds a certification element to verify that the practices and processes are not just implemented but also effective and sustainable. CMMC also integrates additional cybersecurity best practices from other standards, references, and sources.

CMMC provides a more structured and verifiable approach to cybersecurity, aiming to ensure a baseline of security measures across all contractors in the defense industrial base to protect sensitive defense information from cyber threats.

Who Must Comply?

The CMMC maturity model applies to every company within the DoD supply chain, including those in the defense industrial base and those in procurement, construction, or development. This includes prime contractors who interact directly with the DoD and subcontractors who work with contractors to execute DoD contracts. The size of an organization or the amount of involvement with DoD does not matter for compliance. Any organization which wishes to do any work with DoD needs to comply.

What is Protected?

Along with CUI protection, which has been discussed so far, under the CMMC, there is protection for Federal Contract Information (FCI) as well. FCI includes any information the government creates or provides under contract to an organization to provide them with a service or product that is not disclosed to the public.

Certification Levels

There are five levels of CMMC certification that an organization can receive.

1. Level 1: Basic cyber hygiene. This includes

error-free data, proper access controls, obfuscation/encryption for PII, and data quality assurance.

2. Level 2: Intermediate cyber hygiene. At this stage, a company must protect FCI and CUI in a repeatable way. Auditing, media protection, backup and recovery, maintenance, and system integrity are important at this level.

3. Level 3: Good cyber hygiene. Companies at this level typically deal with controlled but unclassified information. It requires a strong plan to deal with cybersecurity threats and the means to carry them out through awareness, training, and incident response.

4. Level 4: Proactive cyber hygiene. This includes all the plans and procedures for protection against threats as described for level 3 and added responsibility for regular assessments and revisions to policies and procedures.

5. Level 5: Advanced cyber hygiene. This level is required for companies dealing with highly desirable information. It includes everything up to level 4 and more sophisticated tools such as anomaly detection and the ability to respond flexibly to threats.

The NIST 800-171 and the CMMC go through changes to keep up with additional laws, regulations, and best security practices in the industry. CMMC is moving away from Model 1.0, and NIST 800-171 will be moving from Revision 2.

Chapter 7: How to Implement Cybersecurity Law Compliance in Your Organization

While many more laws and regulations may apply to an industry or organization based on the niche they operate in, the above chapters cover the most generally applicable laws to provide readers with an idea of the different regulations they might want to consider when going through compliance. But given the complexity and variety of the different laws, how they should be implemented can be an even bigger challenge. This chapter discusses some practical steps to consider when implementing organizational compliance.

What Laws To Comply With?

One of the primary concerns an organization must deal with is knowing which laws to comply with. What laws apply to a specific organization? There is no catch-all answer to this very important question; unfortunately, because of each organization's unique needs and processes, different laws may or may not apply.

The applicability of different laws can be narrowed down based on certain criteria. Some of the questions to be considered when understanding this are:

- What kind of data is being collected and used? Whether PII is being collected or not, how sensitive is the data being collected, if it's payment data or other types of sensitive data, or if the information is personal and could be cause for discrimination if exposed? These are a few things to consider when answering this question.
- Is the organization using a product or service? Whether the organization is providing a product or a service, while this may seem irrelevant on a bigger scale, the organization's approach towards security and privacy and operational policies differ based on whether a product is being sold vs. a service.
- Is there a contract involved and what industry is involved? Suppose the organization is working with government contracts. As discussed in various laws, federal contracts require many extra steps to be taken with respect to privacy and security, as their data and information systems tend to be more sensitive and prone to cyber threats.
- What is the location? Location of the users where the product or service is being offered. As seen in previous chapters, when operating internationally, there are many extra privacy and security regulations that an organization needs to comply with depending on which country the product or service is being offered.

Similarly, many states in the US have their own compliance requirements that must be followed to operate in that state. Where a company is based becomes an important consideration when covering compliance.

- What products or services are an organization using for its processes and operations? This can seem odd, but every organization has certain products and services for smooth functioning. These products and services come with their own security and privacy restrictions, which they must comply with and require for the best functioning of their products and services.

- Are there any special needs for the data or internal security and privacy considerations? How an organization protects its data and information systems is often important when considering compliance. For example, many companies have proprietary software and/or hardware that needs to be covered by IP laws. Similarly, there can be other security and privacy concerns that may require certain compliance.

While this is not an exhaustive list, these questions can form starting points to consider when understanding which laws to comply with. Irrespective of compliance, determining a baseline of security and privacy requirements that an organization must follow and implement is always a good practice.

There is a paper trail that will lead the organization directly to which laws and regulations are applicable.

White papers in the industry or sector will often reference the applicable laws. Academic papers and even vendor data sheets in the industry will cite relevant laws.

Frameworks like the NIST RMF and NIST Cybersecurity framework can provide a sound all-around approach. Apart from compliance, having and following a baseline can protect an organization from monetary losses, reputational damages, and many other side effects of data breaches.

Using the NIST CSF to Ensure Compliance with Laws and Regulations

Navigating the intricate landscape of cybersecurity laws can be daunting. With an array of requirements and benchmarks set by different laws across the globe, the challenge for organizations is to find a universally recognized framework that simplifies and unifies their compliance efforts. The NIST Cybersecurity Framework (NIST CSF) is an efficient tool to meet this need.

Before diving into the merits of the NIST CSF, it's essential to distinguish it from the NIST RMF 800 series. The Risk Management Framework (RMF) 800 series is an exhaustive set of processes tailored mainly for large government systems. While universal in its application, it includes over 1,000 security controls and a very results-based process that can take months or even years to fully implement.

In contrast, the NIST CSF is nimble, adaptable, and designed for entities of all sizes across various industries.

Origin and Purpose of NIST CSF

The NIST Cybersecurity Framework (NIST CSF) was inspired by Executive Order 13636, "Improving Critical Infrastructure Cybersecurity," issued by President Barack Obama on February 12, 2013. This Executive Order directed the NIST to work with stakeholders to develop a voluntary framework to reduce cybersecurity risks to critical infrastructure. The result of this collaboration was the NIST Cybersecurity Framework. Its primary objective is to offer guidance that can thwart or, at the very least, mitigate the impact of cyber-attacks.

Functional Areas of NIST CSF

The framework operates on a business function model, concentrating on five pivotal areas:

- Identify: Recognize and manage cybersecurity risks to systems, assets, data, and capabilities.
- Protect: Implement necessary safeguards to ensure the delivery of critical infrastructure

services.

- Detect: Identify potential cybersecurity events promptly.
- Respond: Take action regarding a detected cybersecurity event.
- Recover: Restore any capabilities or services impaired due to a cybersecurity incident.

For each of these functions, there are specific controls to reinforce the organization's privacy and security posture.

Implementation Tiers of NIST CSF

Understanding that organizations have varied capabilities and resources, the NIST CSF outlines Implementation Tiers that assist entities in gauging their cybersecurity readiness:

- Tier 1 (Partial): Organizational cybersecurity is not formalized. Responses to threats are reactive.
- Tier 2 (Risk-Informed): Management is aware of the risks, but there's no organization-wide approach to addressing them.
- Tier 3 (Repeatable): The organization has a structured risk management process and routinely reviews and updates its cybersecurity practices.
- Tier 4 (Adaptive): The organization adapts its cybersecurity practices based on lessons learned and predictive indicators. It's in a continuous

improvement state.

Aligning with Laws and Regulations

The adaptability and thoroughness of the NIST CSF make it an excellent tool for ensuring compliance with myriad cybersecurity laws. By aligning an organization's security posture with the NIST CSF, entities can be assured that they adhere to best practices, which often meet or exceed regulatory requirements. This alignment aids organizations in reducing compliance gaps, streamlining audit processes, and establishing a solid foundation for expanding their cybersecurity maturity.

While the landscape of cybersecurity laws is vast and ever-evolving, the NIST CSF offers a consistent, structured, and holistic approach to compliance. Adopting and implementing this framework will enhance an organization's security and instill confidence in stakeholders that the organization is resilient against cyber threats.

For more on the NIST CSF, check out the Convocourses series, which dives much deeper into the controls and implementation:

- NIST Cybersecurity Framework for Information Systems Security
- Cyber Security Program and Policy Using NIST CSF

https://www.amazon.com/dp/B0C9376Y8N

Education on Laws and

Compliance

Education and training are other important aspects when preparing for and implementing security and privacy laws for compliance. IT professionals with knowledge of the various laws can make a good compliance plan into a great one. There are often details and nuances within the implementation and processes of the various information systems that non-technical people can miss. But these little details can count when aiming to comply with cyber law. IT professionals trained for compliance are key to filling these gaps and meeting an organization's compliance goals.

Compliance teams should focus on employee training and education as part of ongoing efforts to remain compliant. Often, employee training is part of compliance with many cyber laws, reinforcing the importance of having employee awareness about the different data processing and handling standards. There are several ways to go about employee training for compliance.

- Organizations can design education programs based on data and information system handling patterns and processes.
- Organizations can enlist external training organizations and/or online learning platforms to educate employees and meet the training standards.
- Based on the degree of education an employee

may need, organizations can have options for professional certifications available for employees. Some teams may need a more extensive understanding of compliance by more intensive data and system handling. Several organizations provide professional certifications for specific and generic cyber law education.

After identifying the laws an organization needs to comply with, education can be vital for the implementation of cyber laws correctly.

Risk Assessments

Before implementing a compliance or risk management framework, having an organization-wide risk assessment can be incredibly helpful in determining what to protect, where to allocate resources, and what needs to be improved, updated, or developed to meet compliance requirements. The first step to risk assessment is to assemble a cross-departmental team to cover all aspects within an organization's scope. As a minimum, a risk assessment team should consist of:

- Senior management to provide oversight.
- The chief information security officer to review network architecture.
- A privacy officer to locate personally identifiable information.
- The compliance officer to identify compliance

issues.

- Technical experts from the system team.

Once an optimum team has been assembled, we can follow a five-step approach toward risk assessment.

Step 1: Catalog Information Assets

This includes all of the business's information assets. Systems, processes, as well as the data it processes. This includes all the network assets, software as a service (SaaS), platform as a service (PaaS), infrastructure, third-party vendors, and contractors.

To understand the kind of data that your organization may be handling, it can be good to ponder over these questions:

- What kinds of information are departments collecting?
- Where are they storing that information?
- Where do they send that information?
- From where are they collecting it?
- Which vendors does each department use?
- What access do those vendors have?

Which authentication methods, such as multi-factor authentication, do you use for information access?
- Where, physically, does your company store information?
- Which devices do workforce members use?

- Do remote workers access information? How so?
- Which networks transmit information?
- Which databases store information?
- Which servers collect, transfer, and store data?

Step 2: Categorize the Risk

After listing down all an organization's different assets, the next step is to categorize the risk associated with each asset. This is important because every asset, every vendor, and every piece of data and information can be secure or insecure to varying degrees. For example, some systems may be multiple layers deep into an organization's environment and, therefore, will have a lesser risk of exposure than other systems. Some vendors may already have many security features built into their systems. Because of these differences, categorizing the risk can be a very valuable exercise. When trying to categorize, some of the questions to consider are:

- Which systems, networks, and software are critical to business operations?
- What sensitive information or systems must maintain availability, confidentiality, and integrity?
- What personal information do you store, transmit, or collect that needs to be anonymized in case of an encryption failure?
- Which devices are most at risk of data loss?

- What is the potential for data corruption?
- Which IT systems, networks, and software might cybercriminals target for a data breach?
- What reputation harm might arise from a security incident?
- What financial risks are posed by a potential data breach or data leak?
- What business operation risks would stem from a cybersecurity event?
- Do you have a business continuity plan allowing you to rapidly return to business operations after an IT disruption?

Step 3: Analyze the Risk

The next step should be to analyze the risks associated with each asset and to create a priority framework for them. This primarily depends on two factors: the likelihood or probability of a cybercrime or data breach affecting the asset and the impact damage or loss of said asset can have on the business and different business functions. Based on these two things, we can analyze an asset's actual risk and decide on each asset.

To calculate the risk, an organization can use the formula:

- Risk = (Likelihood of Breach x Impact)/Cost

Here, cost means the monetary losses or expenses incurred to repair or replace the asset. This can help determine, for example, if a resource marked high priority poses a significant risk to an organization's security. This can help to understand which assets or business functions may require more vs. less investment from a security and privacy perspective.

Step 4: Establish Risk Tolerance

The classification of risk above makes it easy to determine risk tolerance. For each asset, based on the risk, it can be determined if the risk is to be accepted, avoided, transferred, or mitigated.

If a risk is accepted, then no action needs to be taken for risk management as, according to the above analysis, it is established that incurring the loss/impact of the risk is the most favorable outcome for the asset.

If a risk is to be avoided, then the actions taken would be to prevent that behavior from happening. This can be through coding safeguards, physical barriers, placing logical layers before the risky asset, asset isolation, or several other ways depending on the asset under consideration.

If a risk is to be transferred, there are several ways to go about it. You can either transfer the processing or handling of an asset to a third-party vendor or to a different business unit within the same organization, one that is better equipped to deal with the risk. Letting somebody with the right resources and expertise handle the risk is more effective than trying to mitigate it.

If a risk is to be mitigated, an organization needs to

develop a protection plan and set up policies to mitigate the risk as and when it appears.

Choosing a Framework

Choosing a framework becomes much simpler with a good understanding of the risk profile. When deciding which framework to use, some of the questions to be considered are:

- **What will be the scope of coverage?** This includes all the different areas within an information system or the different information systems covered within the same framework. Within each pillar, the details that will be covered are also important factors for consideration.
- **What is the existing security culture within the organization? An** organization lacking an existing security perspective among its employees can struggle if many sudden restrictions and regulations are introduced. For this, it is important to ensure that the framework chosen is adaptable for most employees, increasing the likelihood that the regulations will be maintained over time.
- **What, if any, risk management strategies already exist within the organization?** This can help to identify if the framework in consideration will align with the existing policies and plans within the organization.
- **What are the compliance requirements?**

As discussed, not all regulations will apply to all organizations, and knowing which requirements apply and which don't will be a big factor in deciding which framework should be chosen. Consider the industry that the organization is associated with. For example, a company that sells medical equipment is aligned with the health care industry and might consider the HITRUST framework.

Setting and Updating Policies and Controls

Based on the risk tolerance established previously, the policies and controls can be decided for different assets. For example, if the risk is to be mitigated, identify who it will be transferred to and which vendor or business unit will be responsible for mitigating it. Or if a risk is to be mitigated, what actions will be taken in the event of a cyber attack on the asset or before an attack as a preventative measure?

Some examples of controls for risk mitigation are incident response plans and actions and insurance on the risk asset. Whereas preventative measures can include data encryption, security products like firewalls, Virtual Private Networks (VPN), etc.

Keeping these policies and controls up to date should be an ongoing feature when implementing risk management. As risks and their impact continue to evolve, revisiting and updating the controls for better management can often be the difference between a failed and a successful data breach attempt. Regular updates should be built into a good risk management plan to easily adjust policies and controls.

Monitor, Respond, and Iterate

Because threats are evolving almost daily, threat actors always look for new ways to enter an organization. For preventing and mitigating an attack, logging and monitoring can be imperative. Therefore, monitoring and logging should be part of a risk management plan. It also helps to view historical data and identify patterns for future attacks; monitoring and logging can be extremely useful in cybersecurity risk management.

An incident response plan is just as important when planning for risk. It becomes a guidebook for all the steps needed in case of an active incident to prevent further damage than what has already occurred and has proven extremely effective in practice.

Iterating periodically over the risk management plan can identify the existing plan's validity and help identify any gaps, new attack vectors, or new assets that need protection. Just like regular updates of controls and control software can help to keep a strong security posture, periodic iterations can validate the strength of the existing plan.

They should be an important part of the implementation plan.

These are just some things that can be done to implement a process that complies with cybersecurity laws.

Chapter 8: Privacy Laws and Their Impact on Cybersecurity

In discussing the different cyber laws, privacy, and security are often put in the same group and thought of as a collective entity. Organizations often make the mistake of clumping these two together when planning and implementing for compliance. More often than not, the focus is on security, and privacy takes a back seat, or it is assumed that meeting security requirements should be enough to fulfill the privacy requirements as well. Although with the prevalence of GDPR and CCPA, the understanding and awareness around privacy as a distinct aspect within cyber security has increased. There are still significant issues that can come up when privacy goals and security goals conflict with each other.

Privacy Is Not The Same as Security

In theory, it is pretty obvious that privacy and security are not the same thing. But in practice, this distinction can often be blurred. As discussed at the beginning of the book, privacy deals with keeping people's information and information systems private, away from the public eye, or unavailable for general viewing on the internet. Security involves protecting data and information systems, ensuring that it is safe and the integrity of the data and information systems is maintained.

When discussing security laws, the focus is on rules to bring certain data breaches within the law's scope to investigate, identify, and penalize attackers. Organizations and individuals can benefit from cybersecurity laws as they give them a way to address their losses caused by breaches or even an organization's negligence.

When discussing privacy laws, the focus is on individual people and their personal information. The rules are designed to protect individuals from organizational bad practices in data handling and sometimes even intentional data sharing by organizations in an unethical manner.

The perspective behind both types of laws is different. This is quite frequently why security and privacy laws have conflicting interests. For example, security requires that an organization retain information. The information is kept because it can be helpful during investigations to identify the attack source, victims, and other relevant information. However, privacy requires that all personal information, which includes system information and IP addresses, be scrubbed to remove PII. Both requirements become counterintuitive to each other. Maintaining a balance between privacy and security requirements and compliance with both laws can be challenging and intricate.

Common Challenges

Privacy and security are deeply interconnected and face some common challenges.

The Complexity of the Environment

With the fast evolution of technology, the cyber environment is becoming increasingly complex. Options like Single-Sign-On and OAuth credentials, etc., are making data, accounts, and user information interconnected between different apps and organizations. Not only that, with targeted ads and tracking of online activities, the boundaries of who has and uses a person's information are becoming increasingly blurry. With more and more "always on" devices like smart home devices, mobile devices, etc., the online environment has become very complex and difficult to protect both from a privacy and a security perspective.

Sophisticated Threats

Threats and cyber attacks are also becoming more sophisticated. With things like ransomware-as-a-service, there has been a "professionalization" of cybercrime. Rootkits and Advanced Persistent Threats (APTs) are some common examples of extremely sophisticated cyber attacks. As threats evolve, the challenges of privacy and security become more intricate.

The Shift of Threat Landscape to Mobile Devices

There has been an increased use of mobile devices within the past decade, and the capabilities available to these devices have made them an easy target for exploitation. With smart cars, smart TVs, smart refrigerators, and other "internet of things," everything is connected. These devices may seem simplistic, but when exploited, they can be used for sophisticated attacks. The Denial of Service on the Dyn DNS server, which leveraged the Mirai botnet primarily comprised of internet-connected security cameras, is a prime example of the threat mobile devices can pose to an organization.

"Big Data" Paradox

Big data is a large collection of data, often rich in information, useful for organizations to improve customer experiences. Because of this, collected data's size, storage, manipulation, and processing pose new challenges, especially from a security and privacy perspective. This data is as valuable to attackers as it is to organizations. Many PII in this data type create major privacy and security risks.

Compliance Vs. Risk Management

With the increased push for compliance with various laws, companies might take a mechanical approach toward security and privacy. But being compliant will not guarantee a secure environment automatically.

Compliance includes so many governance where tasks are document and management heavy that the actual cyber risks are sometimes sidelined. When done properly, deliberate risk management can imply that compliance obligations are fulfilled. Therefore, how a company approaches compliance and risk management can affect the security and privacy within an organization.

Impact of Privacy Laws on Organizations

Because of mandatory compliance requirements for privacy laws, organizations must maintain certain practices concerning their data and information systems. This has impacted organizations incorporating many otherwise ignored or de-prioritized practices into their system development life-cycle. Before privacy laws, many ethically sound practices were put in the backseat for practical reasons and for keeping up with the market demands. With the introduction of privacy compliance, this problem has been reduced, and the safety of everyone on the internet has increased. Some of the practices which have come up because of this are:

- Regular updates to data privacy policies. Because of consent and notifications compliance requirements, most organizations have had to revise and update their data privacy policies as and when they update how they collect and use data.
- Review of privacy standards. Regularly review and assess their privacy standards to ensure they meet the standards and identify gaps in their risk management.
- Implement best practices. Organizations implement many recommended practices based on legal guidelines to meet the requirements and remain compliant.
- Regular employee training. Often, employee training and education are a part of compliance requirements. This ensures organizations are training their employees and that all employees know the required privacy and security practices they should implement individually. Therefore, creating a more secure environment.

Security and Privacy Together

It may seem like an easy task to enforce security and privacy together. But as discussed repeatedly, privacy and security can often be at odds. Or, the nuances of implementation can differ, making it difficult to implement both optimally. There has been a lot of work put into solving the challenge of security without violating privacy standards, and a lot of common ground has been found in the teams dealing with scrubbing data, analysis on aggregated data instead of individual data, decoupling PII from information essential for enhancing security, and so forth. However, it remains an ongoing effort to ensure that the best possible implementations of privacy and security can be made in tandem while remaining compliant with cyber and privacy laws.

Chapter 9: Cybersecurity Laws and System Certifications

As proof of compliance and to ensure all the mandatory regulations are in place in an organization, several laws and standards require that the organization have a formal written approval from the head of the organization or a certification and accreditation process allowing a system to operate. This is also known as "authorization" and is where the head of the organization accepts the risks in writing. Based on assessment data, they decide their risk tolerance policies, i.e., which risks they will take or reject. National, state and local governments, as well as some industry regulations mandate certification, accreditation, and authorization.

By accrediting an information system, an agency official accepts responsibility for the system's security and is fully accountable for any adverse impacts to the agency if a breach of security occurs. Thus, responsibility and accountability are core principles that characterize security accreditation. Agency officials must have the most complete, accurate, and trustworthy information possible on the security status of their information systems to make timely, credible, risk-based decisions on whether to authorize the operation of those systems.

Certifications In the Law

Here are some laws, regulations and standards that mention certifications and accreditations for compliance:

FISMA

The FISMA law establishes the need for certification and accreditation. While there is no explicit mention of "certification" and "accreditation" in any specific section of the Act, the certification and accreditation process, as interpreted and applied based on the Act, involves reviewing and approving an information system's security controls. The NIST 800 is a guide for the US federal accreditation process in accordance with FISMA.

NIST SP 800-37 Authorization Process

The certification and accreditation process is defined in NIST SP 800-37. Once the system documentation and risk assessment have been completed, the system's controls must be reviewed and certified to function appropriately. Based on the results of the review, the information system is accredited. The process used to be called "certification and accreditation," but now, in the most current NIST 800-37 revisions, it is known as "Assessment and authorization."

Office of Management and Budget (OMB) Circular A-130

Security accreditation is the official management

decision given by a senior agency official to authorize the operation of an information system and to explicitly accept the risk to agency operations, agency assets, or individuals based on the implementation of an agreed-upon set of security controls. OMB Circular A-130, Appendix III requires this process; it provides quality control and challenges managers and technical staff at all levels to implement the most effective security controls possible in an information system, given mission requirements, technical constraints, operational constraints, and cost/schedule constraints.

ISO 27001

ISO 27001 is an international standard offering a systematic and structured framework to establish, implement, operate, monitor, review, maintain, and improve an Information Security Management System (ISMS). The standard delineates guidelines for effectively managing information security within a company.

Contrary to the accreditation process under FISMA, ISO 27001 does entail a rigorous certification process. The organization aspiring for certification is required to conduct a formal risk assessment and then implement security controls appropriate for managing the identified risks. These controls can be selected from the Annex A of the standard or elsewhere, tailored to the organization's specific needs.

The certification process for ISO 27001 involves several stages. Initially, an internal review is performed to comprehend the existing ISMS, followed by a gap analysis to pinpoint areas that need enhancement. The organization then works on the development and implementation of the ISMS, ensuring it is in line with ISO 27001 requirements. Comprehensive documentation is prepared to evidence the establishment and efficient operation of the ISMS.

An internal audit is then conducted to evaluate the ISMS's effectiveness, and any identified non-conformities are addressed through corrective actions. The management reviews the ISMS to ensure it aligns with the organization's objectives and is effective. Necessary adjustments and improvements are made accordingly.

The certification audit is a two-stage process: The first stage involves a documentation review by the certification body, and the second stage is an on-site audit to evaluate the implementation and effectiveness of the ISMS in a real-world scenario. If the organization satisfies the requirements, the ISO 27001 certificate is issued, typically valid for three years and subject to periodic surveillance audits.

The maintenance and continual improvement phase ensures that the ISMS is regularly monitored and updated to remain effective. The organization undergoes periodic surveillance audits to validate ongoing compliance with ISO 27001. A re-certification audit is required after three years to renew the certification.

Though ISO 27001 doesn't employ the exact terminology as used in NIST 800, its comprehensive process of risk assessment, implementation of controls, regular review, and external audit aligns with the core objective of ensuring the organization's information security measures are effective and fitting.

The distinct factor lies in the application scope - while FISMA is mandated for U.S. federal agencies, ISO 27001 is a voluntary standard adopted globally by any organization, though it can be a contractual or regulatory requisite in certain sectors or geographies.

Certifications for PCI DSS

The PCI DSS has a form of certification and accreditation, but it operates differently than FISMA. Instead of being authorized to operate a system after a review by a senior official (as in FISMA), companies must validate their compliance with the PCI DSS annually. This can involve different processes depending on the volume of transactions the company processes and the specific rules of the individual card brands.

Certification Process

A general idea of the process is discussed below.

- **Self-Assessment Questionnaire (SAQ).** Most small to medium businesses will complete an SAQ, a PCI Security Standards Council checklist. The SAQ includes questions related to the security controls that the company has in place.
- **External Vulnerability Scanning.** Companies that handle larger volumes of

transactions must have their systems scanned quarterly by a PCI-approved scanning vendor. The purpose of these scans is to identify vulnerabilities that attackers could exploit.

- **On-Site Audit.** The largest processors of credit card transactions and those that have suffered a breach must also have an on-site audit conducted by a Qualified Security Assessor (QSA) or Internal Security Assessor (ISA).
- **Attestation of Compliance (AOC).** Once the company has completed the appropriate validation process, it must submit an AOC to its acquiring bank and the card brands with which they do business.

So, while the specifics are different, the PCI DSS has a similar assessment and validation process (or "certification and accreditation") to ensure that companies follow the required security practices. However, unlike FISMA, which focuses on government information systems, PCI DSS is focused on the security of credit card data in the private sector.

HIPAA Certification

According to Steve Alder (HIPAA journal, Feb 2023), HIPAA certification is defined as either a point in time accreditation demonstrating an organization has passed a HIPAA compliance audit or a recognition that members of the organization's workforce have achieved the level of HIPAA knowledge required to comply with the organization's policies and procedures. While not mandatory, both are useful accreditations to have. Also, having HIPAA certification does not automatically absolve organizations from negligent practices.

The biggest benefit of getting certified is that if a violation still occurs that results in an OCR investigation, a certificate of HIPAA compliance demonstrates "a reasonable amount of care to abide by the HIPAA Rules." This can be the difference between a HIPAA violation classified as a Tier 1 violation (minimum penalty per violation $120) and a Tier 2 violation (minimum penalty per violation $1.205).

For Business Associates and third-party vendors that deal with data classified under HIPAA, certification demonstrates an intention to operate compliantly, making an organization's services more attractive and reducing the amount of due diligence required before entering into a Business Associate Agreement.

Getting HIPAA certification for the workforce has a similar benefit in that a compliant workforce is less likely to violate HIPAA or make mistakes that could result in data breaches. Similarly, achieving workforce HIPAA certification demonstrates a reasonable amount of care to abide by the HIPAA Rules if an investigation or audit takes place. For compliant individuals, this can foster patient trust and boost their value in the job-competitive market.

Unintentional violations of HIPAA usually occur due to a lack of knowledge, shortcuts being taken "to get the job done," or because a cultural norm of noncompliance has been allowed to develop. Whatever the reason, violations of HIPAA can result in serious repercussions ranging from written warnings to loss of professional accreditation, all of which can be avoided by applying the concepts learned in a certification program.

Certification requirements for Covered Entities, Business Associates, and healthcare workers differ because each must follow the rules. The latest requirements can be found in the certifying authorities at the time of certification.

COPPA Safe Harbor Program

COPPA has a Safe Harbor program, which organizations can submit to the COPPA commission self-regulatory guidelines that implement the rule's protections. The commission can then review the request for "safe harbor" treatment within 180 days of submission. After notice and comment, they can approve the request, making the organization a Safe Harbor organization.

The criteria for approval of self-regulatory guidelines, according to the Code of Federal Regulations, part 312.10, are:

1. Program requirements that ensure operators subject to the self-regulatory program guidelines ("subject operators") provide substantially the same or greater protections for children.
2. An effective, mandatory mechanism for independently assessing subject operators' compliance with the self-regulatory program guidelines. At a minimum, this mechanism must include a comprehensive review by the safe harbor program, to be conducted not less than annually, of each subject operator's information policies, practices, and representations. An independent enforcement program, such as a seal program, can provide the assessment mechanism required under this paragraph.
3. Disciplinary actions for subject operators' non-compliance with self-regulatory program guidelines. This performance standard may be satisfied by:
   a Mandatory public reporting of any action taken against subject operators by the industry group issuing the self-regulatory guidelines;
   b Consumer redress;
   c Voluntary payments to the United States Treasury in connection with an industry-directed program for violators of the self-regulatory guidelines;
   d Referral to the Commission of operators who engage in a pattern or practice of

violating the self-regulatory guidelines.

GDPR Certification

The EU does not define a specific certification to be obtained for compliance with GDPR; rather, it defines rules and regulations for the certification companies to follow before providing a certification of GDPR compliance. These certifications are encouraged to be established at the union level for maximum uniformity in compliance.

According to Art. 42 GDPR - Certification - GDPR.eu (2018), the following guidelines are provided for certification organizations:

1. The Member States, the supervisory authorities, the Board, and the Commission shall encourage, in particular at the Union level, the establishment of data protection certification mechanisms and data protection seals and marks to demonstrate compliance with this regulation of processing operations by controllers and processors. The needs of micro, small, and medium-sized enterprises shall be considered.

2. In addition to adherence by controllers or processors subject to this Regulation, data protection certification mechanisms, seals, or marks may be established to demonstrate the existence of appropriate safeguards provided by

controllers or processors that are not subject to this Regulation. Such controllers or processors shall make binding and enforceable commitments, via contractual or other legally binding instruments, to apply those appropriate safeguards, including about the rights of data subjects.

3. The certification shall be voluntary and available via a transparent process.

4. According to this Article, a certification does not reduce the responsibility of the controller or the processor for compliance with this Regulation. It is without prejudice to the competent supervisory authorities' tasks and powers.

5. A certification shall be issued by the certification bodies or the competent supervisory authority based on criteria approved by that competent supervisory authority. Where the Board approves the criteria may result in a common certification, the European Data Protection Seal.

6. The controller or processor that submits its processing to the certification mechanism shall provide the certification body, or where applicable, the competent supervisory authority, with all information and access to its processing activities necessary to conduct the certification procedure.

7. Certification shall be issued to a controller or processor for three years. It may be renewed under the same conditions, provided the relevant criteria are met. Certification shall be withdrawn, as applicable, by the certification bodies or the competent supervisory authority where the criteria for the certification are not or

are no longer met.

8. The Board shall collate all certification mechanisms and data protection seals and marks in a register and make them publicly available by any appropriate means.

Chapter 10: Future of Cybersecurity Laws

As technology evolves, cyber security and privacy requirements will continue to grow and change. New challenges are coming up daily as the world becomes increasingly interconnected and more and more activities happen online. Discussed next are some things predicted to change the landscape of cybersecurity and privacy in the next decade.

Cybersecurity for the Internet of Things

According to Ahmed Banafa (OpenMind BBVA, April 2023), the rise of the Internet of Things (IoT) is also set to have a major impact on the future of cybersecurity. IoT devices are becoming increasingly common and are often used to control critical systems and infrastructure. However, many IoT devices have poor security features and can be easily compromised by cybercriminals. As a result, organizations will need to implement better security measures to protect against IoT-related cyber threats. As it is, many laws have started including amendments to add IoT security to their definitions.

- The EU recently added measures to include IoT privacy rules to GDPR. The EU Cybersecurity Act, effective June 27, 2019, became law in the European Union and the UK, which includes regulations for IoT devices. The NIS Directive (IoT infrastructure) became effective on May 24, 2018, in the EU and the UK.
- In the US, the IoT Cybersecurity Improvement Act of 2020 gives NIST the authority to manage cybersecurity risk arising from IoT devices and develop risk management frameworks.
- The California IoT cybersecurity law became effective in January 2020 and aims to manage cybersecurity risks.

Under the IoT Act of 2020, NIST has released guidelines called "Recommendations for IoT Device Manufacturers: Foundational Activities and Core Device Cybersecurity Capability Baseline," which aims to integrate secure development into IoT device SDLC. It defines six simple features that consumers should look for:

- A unique identifier (a serial number, for instance)
- The ability to change firmware configuration
- Data Protection
- Secure access to administrative control
- The ability to update firmware and software
- Cybersecurity event logging

Child Privacy Laws

As children venture online more and more, this activity is often unsupervised. It is next to impossible to monitor every online activity a child does, given there is such a wide variety of information available, from education to entertainment, all aimed at children. COPPA is a great first step towards protecting the privacy of minors online. Still, as technology evolves, it may not be enough to protect the different forms of online interaction that are coming up.

Children's or minors' privacy is a bigger concern because they are more susceptible to suggestions and not psychologically equipped to deal with different stressors and influences. Cyberbullying, blackmailing, and fear tactics are some of the things that would affect minors more severely than adults. With newer avenues of online interactions appearing, there are many more avenues for threat actors to collect, steal, and sell minor's information online. With time, amendments will have to be made to COPPA, and new laws will be introduced to protect minors from the harmful effects of information oversharing.

AI Laws

Governments and industries are adjusting to artificial intelligence capabilities. With the ability to mimic and remix creative works, copywrite is a concern. Since AI can be used as a tool in cyber attacks, the level of sophistication will need AI cyber defense backed by cyber law.

Governments and industry are drafting regulation to deal with AI.

As of 2023, the influx of Artificial Intelligence (AI) has triggered a global reevaluation and adaptation of legal frameworks and regulatory guidelines. AI's unprecedented growth and expanding capabilities necessitate this reassessment to manage potential ethical, privacy, and security challenges.

Copyright Concerns:

AI's ability to create, mimic, and remix creative works has ushered in new complexities in copyright laws. Traditional copyright frameworks are being challenged, as AI-generated content blurs the lines of authorship and originality. The legal systems are now grappling with questions like - Who owns the copyright of AI-generated content? Is it the creator of the AI, the user, or does it remain unowned? Legislators and policymakers are in the throes of establishing legal precedents and modifying existing copyright laws to address these concerns, ensuring that rights and royalties are fairly attributed and protected.

AI in Cybersecurity:

With AI becoming a potent tool in cyber-attacks, cybersecurity laws are also undergoing significant transformation. The sophistication of these attacks demands an equally advanced AI-backed defense system. Cyber laws are being updated to incorporate requirements for advanced security protocols, mandatory AI ethical standards, and accountability measures to counter AI-enabled cyber threats effectively. The role of AI in both cyber offenses and defenses is leading to a nuanced legal landscape where adaptability and anticipation of emerging threats are key.

Regulatory Frameworks:

Governments and industries worldwide are collaboratively drafting new regulations to address the multifaceted challenges posed by AI. These regulations aim to ensure that AI is developed and used in ways that are ethical, safe, and in the interest of the public. They are focusing on transparency, accountability, and fairness to mitigate biases and discrimination in AI applications. The establishment of international AI ethics standards is also on the agenda to foster global cooperation and ensure that AI benefits humanity as a whole.

Privacy and Data Protection:

AI's extensive reliance on data has also spotlighted privacy and data protection issues. Existing data protection laws like GDPR in Europe and CCPA in California are being revisited to incorporate specific provisions for AI. These include stricter consent requirements for data processing, transparency in automated decision-making processes, and the rights of individuals to opt out of AI-driven decisions.

Ethical AI:

Ethics in AI is another dominant theme. There's a growing consensus on the need for ethical guidelines that govern AI development and deployment. Ethical AI seeks to ensure that technology is used in a manner that is just, fair, and respects human rights. Initiatives to develop principles and guidelines for ethical AI are underway, with participation from a diverse range of stakeholders including governments, international organizations, civil society, and the private sector.

AI Governance:

AI governance is also emerging as a critical aspect, with frameworks being established to monitor and evaluate AI's impact on society continuously. These governance structures are designed to be dynamic, adapting to the rapid evolution of AI technologies and their applications.

The intersection of AI and law is evolving rapidly, shaped by ongoing technological advancements and the emerging challenges they present. Balancing innovation with ethical, security, and privacy concerns is central to the ongoing discourse, necessitating a multidimensional approach that encompasses legal, ethical, and technological perspectives. Adaptation and anticipation are the watchwords, with laws and regulations crafted to be as dynamic and innovative as AI itself.

Conclusion

Cybersecurity and privacy laws have become imperative in today's landscape with increasing activities online. Practically anything of value that happens tends to happen online as well. With this hyper-connectivity, IT professionals are responsible for compliance and management of security and privacy. A comprehensive knowledge and understanding of the different cyber laws can go a long way when incorporating compliance into the SDLC. Increased connectivity also means national boundaries are blurred, and everyone is dealing with data worldwide. This makes compliance with international regulations of utmost importance. Given the amount of different laws and regulations, it can feel overwhelming to meet compliance requirements. However, a step-by-step approach with the support of the different risk management frameworks can be of immense value and simplify many requirements into bite-size implementable solutions.

With that said, how a risk management framework or a compliance requirement is implemented can make or break the security and privacy of an organization. More often than not, security measures are available but are not implemented or enabled in a manner that becomes useless for security. When using third-party tools, this can be even more relevant. Enabling and configuring certain features and rules can be a challenge in itself.

Training and education on the various security tools and choosing those that fit the best with an organization's needs is an important exercise that should be done by any team looking to use tools like firewalls, IDS, IPS, and others from third-party vendors.

Education of non-IT professionals on the proper use of the various tools they interact with daily is also crucial. End users are often the most insecure aspect in the chain of command with security and privacy. Improper use of technology is a bigger risk than it seems when considering security and privacy. Users should be trained and made aware of the proper use of different technology and have explained the implications of careless actions over the internet to the organization. This can help with more responsible online conduct in a professional and personal environment, improving the security posture of the organization and the individual.

All stakeholders should be involved in risk management as an ongoing endeavor and participate in reviewing and updating security and privacy policies.

With the evolving threat landscape, it is difficult to anticipate what security and privacy will look like after a decade. IoT devices and smart home appliances have introduced a factor of risk that was previously unanticipated. The fact that devices with seemingly limited capabilities can still be exploited and used to launch larger attacks gives an idea of how sophisticated cyber attackers can be. With the involvement of nation-state-funded cybercrime groups, the threat is not just of monetary loss or data loss but also to national security. With the increased involvement of AI in business functions, new threats are being introduced every day as attackers try to fool or break the technology for their benefit. Keeping ahead of the curve is becoming more of a challenge as technology is evolving in multiple directions, and the competition to bring new technology to market is creating an artificial rush. Keeping security and privacy at the forefront during the SDLC is imperative as much as releasing patches for newly found vulnerabilities is. The perspective of IT professionals should be security first to make secure development a reality.

This shift begins with incorporating different risk management frameworks, compliance certifications, and employee training. Companies are prioritizing security and privacy and maintaining compliance. New laws and regulations to match up with emerging threats and amendments to old laws are helping organizations maintain the best possible security posture. White-hat hackers are uncovering different vulnerabilities and supporting organizations in maintaining the organization's security and privacy postures. Even as the threats evolve, organizations and governments vigilantly update themselves to match up.

References

7 Ways To Build A Cybersecurity Compliance Plan. (n.d.). Www.complianceonline.com.

https://www.complianceonline.com/resources/cybersecurity

-compliance-plan.html

9-48.000 - Computer Fraud and Abuse Act. (2015, February

19).   Www.justice.gov.

https://www.justice.gov/jm/jm-9-48000-computer-

fraud#:~:text=The%20Computer%20Fraud%20and%20Ab

use

Art. 42 GDPR - Certification - GDPR.eu. (2018, November

14). GDPR.eu.

https://gdpr.eu/article-42-data-protection-certification/

Banafa, A. (2023, April 3). *The Future of Cybersecurity:*

Predictions   and   Trends.   OpenMind.

https://www.bbvaopenmind.com/en/technology/digital-

world/future-of-cybersecurity-predictions-trends/

Best Practices for Building a Cybersecurity Compliance Plan. (2020, October 6). www.SecurityScorecard. https://securityscorecard.com/blog/building-a-cybersecurity-compliance-plan/

Bureau of Justice Assistance. (n.d.). *Electronic Communications Privacy Act of 1986 (ECPA)*. Bureau of Justice Assistance. https://bja.ojp.gov/program/it/privacy-civil-liberties/authorities/statutes/1285

Castagna, Rich. (2021). *What is GDPR? An Overview of GDPR Compliance and Conditions*. WhatIs.com. https://www.techtarget.com/whatis/definition/General-Data-Protection-Regulation-GDPR

Centers for Disease Control and Prevention. (2019, February 21). *Health insurance portability and accountability act of 1996(HIPAA)|CDC*. Www.cdc.gov. https://www.cdc.gov/phlp/publications/topic/hipaa.html#:~:text=The%20Health%20Insurance%20Portability%20and

Charles, F. (2023, February 22). *What Is DFARS and What Does it Mean to Be Compliant?* Blog.charlesit.com. https://blog.charlesit.com/what-is-dfars-and-what-does-it-mean-to-be-compliant

Chin, K. (2023, January 12). *Top 20 Worst HIPAA Violation Cases in History | UpGuard.* Www.upguard.com. https://www.upguard.com/blog/worst-hipaa-violation-cases

Chipeta, C. (2023, March 2). *Top 8 Healthcare Cybersecurity Regulations and Frameworks | UpGuard.* Www.upguard.com. https://www.upguard.com/blog/cybersecurity-regulations-and-frameworks-healthcare

Consumer information on Anthem Blue Cross data breach. (n.d.). Www.insurance.ca.gov. https://www.insurance.ca.gov/0400-news/0100-press-releases/anthemcyberattack.cfm

Coos, A. (2019, February). *Data Protection in Japan: All You Need to Know about APPI.* Endpoint Protector Blog.

https://www.endpointprotector.com/blog/data-protection-in-japan-appi/

COPPA Safe Harbor Program. (2015, January 7). Federal Trade Commission. https://www.ftc.gov/enforcement/coppa-safe-harbor-program#:~:text=The%20Children%27s%20Online%20Privacy%20Protection

Cyber Resilience Act | Shaping Europe's digital future. (2022, September 15). Digital- Strategy.ec.europa.eu. https://digital-strategy.ec.europa.eu/en/library/cyber-resilience-act

DDoS attacks on Dyn. (2022, July 14). Wikipedia. https://en.wikipedia.org/wiki/DDoS_attacks_on_Dyn

De Groot, J. (2023, May 6). *What is GLBA Compliance? Understanding the Data Protection Requirements of the Gramm-Leach-Bliley Act.* Digital Guardian. https://www.digitalguardian.com/blog/what-glba-compliance-understanding-data-   protection-requirements-gramm-leach-bliley-act

DFARS Compliance: The Practical Guide for DoD Contractors. (n.d.). Www.cuicktrac.com. https://www.cuicktrac.com/dfars-compliance

Federal Information Security Modernization Act | CISA. (n.d.). Www.cisa.gov. https://www.cisa.gov/topics/cyber-threats-and-advisories/federal-information-security-modernization-act#:~:text=Overview

Federal Register :: Request Access. (2013, January 17). Unblock.federalregister.gov. https://www.ecfr.gov/current/title-16/chapter-I/subchapter-C/part-312

Fruhlinger, J. (2021, May 31). *HITRUST explained: One framework to rule them all.* CSO Online. https://www.csoonline.com/article/3619534/hitrust-explained-one-framework-to-rule-   them-all.html

Garg, R. (2021, October 24). *All you need to know about the*

Children's Online Privacy Protection Act (COPPA). IPleaders. https://blog.ipleaders.in/all-you-need-to-know-about-the-childrens-online-privacy- protection-act-coppa/

Group, G. L. (n.d.). *International Comparative Legal Guides.* International Comparative Legal Guides International Business Reports. Retrieved June 18, 2023, from https://iclg.com/practice-areas/cybersecurity-laws-and-regulations/1-why-ai-is-the-future- of-cybersecurity

GSNA), R. R. (CISSP, CCSFP. (2023, March 15). *HITRUST CSF (Common Security Framework): A Beginner's Guide.* Linford & Company LLP. https://linfordco.com/blog/hitrust-csf-framework/

Halbleib, M. (n.d.). *What is HITRUST Compliance?* SecurityMetrics. https://www.securitymetrics.com/blog/what-hitrust-compliance

Hayes, A. (2022, July 21). *Class Action*. Investopedia.

https://www.investopedia.com/terms/c/classaction.asp

HIPAA Explained. (2018). HIPAA Journal.

https://www.hipaajournal.com/hipaa-explained/

Hreben, M. (2022, January 7). *3 Considerations Before Choosing a Risk Management Framework*. Security Vitals.

https://securityvitals.com/3-considerations-before-choosing-a-risk-management-framework/

https://www.facebook.com/thehackernews. (2022, December 9). *What Stricter Data Privacy Laws Mean for Your Cybersecurity Policies*. The Hacker News.

https://thehackernews.com/2022/12/what-stricter-data-privacy-laws-mean.html

IoT Cybersecurity: regulating the Internet of Things. (2021, June). Thales Group.

https://www.thalesgroup.com/en/markets/digital-identity-and-security/iot/inspired/iot- regulations

Journal, H. (2023, February 19). *What is HIPAA Certification? Updated 2023*. HIPAA Journal. https://www.hipaajournal.com/what-is-hipaa-certification/

Joyce, K. (2022, September 28). *DoD Cybersecurity Requirements: Tips for Compliance*. https://Blog.netwrix.com/. https://blog.netwrix.com/2022/09/28/dod_cyber_security_r equirements/

Karp, B. (2015). *Federal Guidance on the Cybersecurity Information Sharing Act of 2015*. Harvard.edu. https://corpgov.law.harvard.edu/2016/03/03/federal- guidance-on-the-cybersecurity- information-sharing- act-of-2015/

Kastner, E. (2020, April 28). *The Future of Cyber Security Law*. Www.soscanhelp.com. https://www.soscanhelp.com/blog/the-future-of-cyber- security-law

Kelley, K. (2018, December). *What is compliance audit? -*

Definition from WhatIs.com. SearchCIO.

https://www.techtarget.com/searchcio/definition/complianc
e-audit

Kin, L. C., Drew, & Napier. (2021, October 28). *Singapore:
Cybersecurity.* Lexology.

https://www.lexology.com/library/detail.aspx?g=f5adb291-
7dc9-4ade-af4b-   4d3cda9c9c29

Kumari, V. (n.d.). *CYBER LAW -I.* Retrieved June 18, 2023,
from

https://udrc.lkouniv.ac.in/Content/DepartmentContent/SM_
aec24985-8fe2-4500-8414-   85de787ab1e6_30.pdf

Landi, H. (2020, September 30). *Anthem to pay $39M to
state AGs to settle landmark 2015 data   breach.*
FierceHealthcare.

https://www.fiercehealthcare.com/tech/anthem-to-pay-
39m-to-state-ags-to-settle-   landmark-2015-data-breach

Mahawar, S. (2021, August 9). *Technological developments
and social impact caused by cyber   law.* IPleaders.

https://blog.ipleaders.in/technological-developments-social-impact-caused-cyber-law/

Mahawar, S. (2022, August 24). *Information Technology Act, 2000*. IPleaders. https://blog.ipleaders.in/information-technology-act-2000/

NASA Contractor Cybersecurity Requirements | VSG. (n.d.). Vogel, Slade & Goldstein LLP. Retrieved June 18, 2023, from https://www.vsg-law.com/practice-areas/cybersecurity-whistleblower-lawyer/nasa-   contractor-requirements/

NIST. (2016, November 30). *About the RMF - NIST Risk Management Framework | CSRC | CSRC*. CSRC | NIST. https://csrc.nist.gov/projects/risk-management/about-rmf

NPD   2810.1F -   main. (2022,   January   21). Nodis3.Gsfc.nasa.gov. https://nodis3.gsfc.nasa.gov/displayDir.cfm?t=NPD&c=2810&s=1E

O'Neil, M. (2001, December). *Cybercrime Dilemma: Is it*

Possible to Guarantee Both Security and   Privacy?

Brookings; Brookings.

https://www.brookings.edu/articles/cybercrime-dilemma-is-

it-possible-to-guarantee-both-security-and-privacy/

Office of the Privacy Commissioner of Canada. (2015,

February 12). *Privacy and Cyber Security.* Www.priv.gc.ca.

https://www.priv.gc.ca/en/opc-actions-and-

decisions/research/explore-privacy-

research/2014/cs_201412/

PART   1852—SOLICITATION   PROVISIONS   AND

CONTRACT CLAUSES | Acquisition.GOV. (2015).

Acquisition.gov; ACQ.gov.

https://www.acquisition.gov/nfs/part-

1852%E2%80%94solicitation-provisions-and-contract-

clauses#Section_1852_204_76_T48_6042344114

PCI DSS: taking payment security seriously | IT Governance

USA.   (n.d.).   Itgovernanceusa.com.

https://www.itgovernanceusa.com/pci_dss

PDPC | Data Protection Obligations. (n.d.). Www.pdpc.gov.sg.

https://www.pdpc.gov.sg/Overview-of-PDPA/The-Legislation/Personal-Data-Protection-Act/Data-Protection-Obligations

Personal Information Security Specification | Global law firm | Norton Rose Fulbright. (2018, January).

https://Www.nortonrosefulbright.com/En/Knowledge/Publications/Imported/2018/07/18/05.

https://www.nortonrosefulbright.com/en/knowledge/publications/f959f04d/personal-information-security-specification

Privacy vs. Security: Understanding the Difference. (2022, January28).   Www.auditboard.com.

https://www.auditboard.com/blog/privacy-vs-security/

Reuters, T. (n.d.). *Practical Law UK Signon*. Signon.thomsonreuters.com.

https://uk.practicallaw.thomsonreuters.com/3-508-5021?transitionType=Default&contextData=(sc.Default)

&firstPage=true

RiskOptics. (2022, November 22). *5 Steps to Performing a Cybersecurity Risk Assessment.* Reciprocity. https://reciprocity.com/blog/5-steps-to-performing-a-cybersecurity-risk-assessment/

Security, C. (n.d.). *DFARS Compliance in 5 Minutes: The Definitive Guide to NIST SP 800-171.* Www.cybersaint.io. Retrieved June 18, 2023, from https://www.cybersaint.io/cybersecurity/frameworks-and-standards/dfars

Sharma, A. (2021, July 20). *Cyber Laws in different countries.* Medium. https://wizardingcodes.medium.com/cyber-laws-in-different-countries-505524434229

siddhi2420. (2020, May 29). *Information Technology Act, 2000 (India).* GeeksforGeeks. https://www.geeksforgeeks.org/information-technology-act-2000-india/

Swinhoe, D. (2019, November 4). The biggest data breach fines, penalties and settlements so far. *CSOonline.* https://www.csoonline.com/article/3410278/the-biggest-data-breach-fines-penalties-and-   settlements-so-far.html

The HIPAA Privacy Rule. (2021, February 4). Www.accountablehq.com. https://www.accountablehq.com/post/the-hipaa-privacy-rule

Tierney, M. (2021, June 18). *What Is Cybersecurity Maturity Model Certification (CMMC)?* https://Blog.netwrix.com/. https://blog.netwrix.com/2021/06/18/cybersecurity-maturity-model-certification- compliance/

Tunggal, A. (2022, June 7). *What is FISMA? FISMA Compliance Requirements | UpGuard.* www.upguard.com. https://www.upguard.com/blog/fisma

Tunggal, A. T. (2023, May 20). *What is SOX Compliance? Overview, Requirements, and Controls | UpGuard.* www.upguard.com.

https://www.upguard.com/blog/sox-compliance

Understanding the California Consumer Privacy Act (CCPA). (n.d.). Legal.thomsonreuters.com. https://legal.thomsonreuters.com/en/insights/articles/understanding-california-consumer- privacy-act#:~:text=The%20CCPA%20grants%20consumers%20several

UpCounsel. (2013). *Cyber Law: Everything You Need to Know*. UpCounsel. https://www.upcounsel.com/cyber-law

Verma, A. (2020, March 29). *Data Protection and Privacy Policies in Cyber Law*. IPleaders. https://blog.ipleaders.in/data-protection-and-privacy-policies-in-cyber-law/

Wagner, J. (2017, June). *China's Cybersecurity Law: What*

You Need to Know.   Thediplomat.com.

https://thediplomat.com/2017/06/chinas-cybersecurity-law-

what-you-need-to-know/

What global cyber and cybersecurity regulations are there?

| CUBE. (2023, February 22).   CUBE Global.

https://www.cube.global/resource/what-global-cyber-and-

cybersecurity-regulations-are-   there/

What is HITRUST? (n.d.). Www.schneiderdowns.com.

https://www.schneiderdowns.com/cybersecurity/what-is-

hitrust#:~:text=The%20HITRUST%20Common%20Securi

ty%20Framework

What is NIST SP 800-171? How to stay compliant in 2021 -

Titania.   (2021).   Titania.com.

https://www.titania.com/resources/guides/nist-800-171/

Wikipedia Contributors. (2019, February 21). *Facebook–*

Cambridge Analytica data scandal. Wikipedia;

Wikimedia Foundation.

https://en.wikipedia.org/wiki/Facebook%E2%80%93Camb

ridge_Analytica_data_scandal

Wikipedia Contributors. (2021, February 2). *Cybersecurity Law of the People's Republic of China.* Wikipedia; Wikimedia Foundation. https://en.wikipedia.org/wiki/Cybersecurity_Law_of_the_People %27s_Republic_of_China

Wong, J. C. (2019, March 18). *The Cambridge analytica scandal changed the world – but it didn't change facebook.* The Guardian. https://www.theguardian.com/technology/2019/mar/17/the-cambridge-analytica-scandal- changed-the-world-but-it-didnt-change-facebook

www.ingramcontent.com/pod-product-compliance
Lightning Source LLC
Chambersburg PA
CBHW061449150726
47987CB00001B/390